CHURCH
NEEDLEWORK

1 Eucharistic set of green vestments: Chasuble,
dalmatic and tunicle (illustrated) and stoles.
St Mark's Church, Philadelphia, USA

CHURCH NEEDLEWORK

BERYL DEAN

B T Batsford Limited London

ISBN 0 7134 64054

Typeset by Latimer Trend & Company Ltd
Plymouth
and printed in Great Britain by
Butler and Tanner Ltd, Frome

for the publishers
B T Batsford Limited
4 Fitzhardinge Street
London W1H 0AH

CONTENTS

ACKNOWLEDGMENT TO FIRST EDITION

For the assistance given to me by the Central Council for the Care of Churches and to the Benedictines of Prinknash Abbey, I am most grateful. I also want to extend my most sincere thanks to Miss K M Reynolds, Hon. Sacristan, Southwark Cathedral, and Mr W I Croome, C.B.E., J.P., M.A., F.S.A., for their help and to Mrs P Scrase for allowing four of her drawings to be reproduced.

London 1961   Beryl Dean

ACKNOWLEDGMENT TO 1990 EDITION

I would thank all those who have so willingly supplied illustrations of their work for this new edition, acknowledgment to whom is made in the relevant captions. I also thank the following photographers for permission to include their photographs:

Keith Collie for figure 124
Malcolm Crowthers, London, for figure 144
Sam Kelly for figures 93 and 94
Belinda Montague for figures 66 and 67
Walter Schiff for figure 1
Ian Southwood for figure 88

and the following for permission to illustrate embroideries in their possession:

The Dean and Chapter of Salisbury Cathedral for figures 66, 67, 88, 93 and 94
The Dean and Chapter of Westminster Abbey for figures 100 and 144
His Grace the Archbishop of Canterbury for figure 124.

I would also thank Father Charles Moore of St Mark's Church, Philadelphia, USA, for his help in making possible the photography for figure 1, and I am indebted to Mrs A J Cherney for her expertise in typing the text.

London 1990   Beryl Dean

PREFACE

THIRTY years have elapsed since the first edition of *Church Needlework* was published. There is now an even greater need for a thoroughly practical book – one which concentrates upon giving clear instructions for the construction of vestments and soft furnishings for the church.

In the intervening time there has been an exciting development in the approach to design for embroidery in religion. Much has been achieved towards raising the idea of embroidery as a craft to the level of fine art.

The influence of the more adventurous and creative ideas produced in Art and Technical Colleges can be seen in the work which amateurs produce (sometimes, regretfully, without a real understanding).

The interest in, and use of, machine embroidery has developed and increased in importance to an extent which would have seemed impossible years ago.

This new edition of *Church Needlework* deals especially with making-up and with altar linen, both subjects somewhat neglected. The format of the book has been changed; there are additions to the text, and more new illustrations. There are extra up-dated working diagrams, all of which should prove useful to the church embroiderer.

The section dealing with all aspects of embroidery is placed at the end of the book; this includes white linen embroidery. Precise directions and information is given on the various techniques used in hand embroidery and the relation to vestments and furnishings.

London 1990   Beryl Dean

INTRODUCTION TO
FIRST EDITION

The development of new building materials and changed circumstances have influenced the form of present-day church architecture; and there is real creativity in the church arts, such as stained glass. But it is still the exception, rather than the general practice, for the designer with vision to be commissioned to design for the embroideries. There is an ever-increasing interest in the subject and more and more artist-craftswomen are working in the idiom of today, but can enough really good, vital, sincere embroidery be produced? Do churchmen themselves, or the generous donors, or the kindly embroideresses who volunteer to produce furnishings and vestments, understand and accept the trends in contemporary ecclesiastical needlework or do they still hanker after the familiar, often repeated, traditional work, probably technically perfect of its type, but lacking in liveliness and impact?

Tradition and prejudice take time to combat so that the introduction of a more vital approach to church embroidery presents a challenge. Yet it is for the church that we should produce the very best work which is typical of our day; therefore, the need is for better designs, imaginative interpretation and functional construction, befitting to the sacred purpose.

London 1961   Beryl Dean

THE EUCHARISTIC VESTMENTS

PRIORITY will be given to the basic principles which apply to the construction of church vestments, altar linen and soft furnishings. These will be dealt with in detail before the information concerning the embroidered decoration is given. However interesting this may be, its impact can be spoilt if the making up looks clumsy and amateurish. A garment which hangs well, though made of plain fabric, can be preferable, however splendid the embroidery.

The importance of the finish may seem boring yet there is a sense of satisfaction when a perfect vestment has been created.

The full set or *High Mass set* of vestments consists of: the chasuble, dalmatic, tunicle, two stoles, chalice and humeral veils, and burse. Cope or copes are optional. There should be a set in each of the liturgical colours. (See also page 132.)

A *Low Mass set* comprises: chasuble, stole, chalice veil and burse.

For a *Benediction set* there is a cope, stole, burse and humeral veil, with or without a monstrance cover.

The vestments illustrated in *figure 2* are in the order in which they are put on by the priest.

1 *The amice*, which is worn round the neck,

2 The Eucharistic Vestments

to fill up with its folds the space caused by the size of the neck of the chasuble (the apparel should not be omitted from the amice).

2 *The alb*, a long tunic of linen, has apparels at the wrist and at the lower edges of

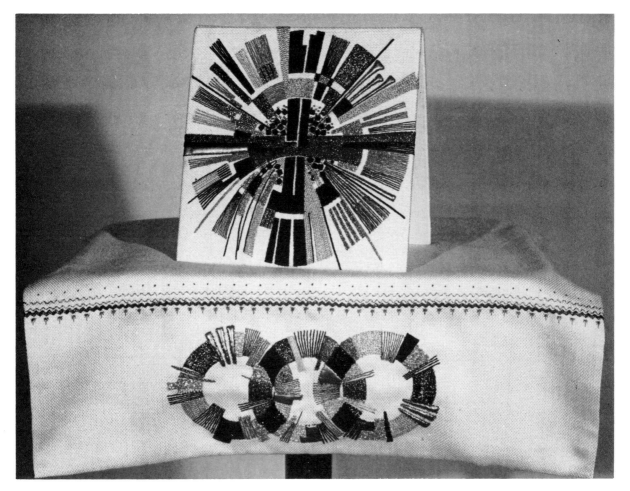

3 Part of a Festal set of vestments for All Saints' Church, Newland, Gloucestershire. Designed by Beryl Dean carried out as a corporate project
(a) Burse and Veil worked by Sister Kathleen sm and Adéle Fraser

the skirts, front and back. The alb is also worn by the celebrant and by the epistoler and gospeller.

3 *The girdle* confines the alb at the waist. It is usually of a white linen rope, with tassels, and is about 3.6 m long.

4 *The stole*: bishops wear it with the ends hanging straight; priests, when celebrating, wear it with the ends crossed and kept in place by the girdle; and deacons wear the stole over the left shoulder and tied under the right arm.

5 *The maniple*, no longer required, was worn over the left wrist.

6 Lastly, the priest, when vesting, puts on the chasuble.

When fully vested, a bishop wears, in addition, under a chasuble, a thin silk dalmatic over a tunicle; this is the reason for the sleeves of the latter being narrower. There are, too, the gloves and the cope and mitre.

The dalmatic is worn by the deacon, and the tunicle by the subdeacon. The deacon wears the stole, but both have also the amice.

Fabrics
The same material is generally used for the whole Eucharistic set. It should be of a weight which will drape well. Some fabrics are too stiff to hang in good folds.

Generally a fairly smooth surface is pre-

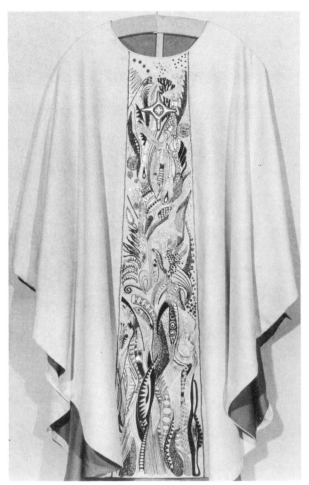

(b) Chasuble (front view) worked by Jenny Miskin

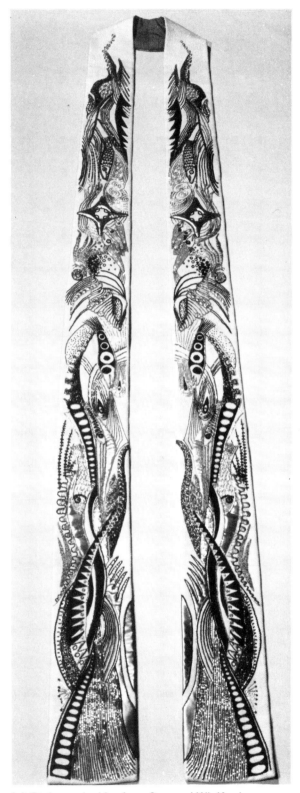

(c) Stole worked by Joan Carr and Winifred Petheram

ferable when there is to be embroidery, but when the beauty depends upon the material only, an interesting texture or slight woven design, or, if used with discretion, a patterned textile can look beautiful. A printed or sprayed effect can be combined with other techniques.

A good, possibly inexpensive unpretentious material, in an interesting colour, for example a dupion, is always preferable to a showy, shiny fabric.

The designs of conventional damasks and brocades belong to the past. Copies, woven in man-made fibres, usually in a limited range of so-called liturgical colours (white, red, purple and green) really should be avoided. The pattern conflicts

4 Part of a set of Paschal Vestments designed by Katarin Privett, for St Mary's Church, Bridport, Dorset

with embroidery not only in character but in style, and renders it unsuitable as a background.

Fabrics of the twentieth century are exciting, the range has developed enormously, and there are Thai, Indian and Chinese silks in wonderful colours, but they are expensive. Or there are Sekers and Sanderson textiles which are more moderately priced. There is an excellent colour range in these and similar textiles (some do crease and should not be used for vestments). Many dress materials are also useful and are well suited to the contemporary idiom. Some fine wools can be used. For the tropics linen is practicable, it is also frequently used during Passion Tide.

The 152 cm wide silk or silk and cotton woven for the purpose are perfect, as they hang well and cut economically.

Shantung, the softer poults, silks, some rayons and Jap silk are all suitable as linings. Unfortunately the colours of some viscose lining material are not stable, but its width is a great advantage, and it is soft. See list of suppliers at the end of the book.

THE CHASUBLE

Design

As a part of the set of Eucharistic vestments, the chasuble conforms to the colour for the season, and the decoration is treated as a part of the whole scheme. The full or Gothic shape is more generally in use now, and all chasubles are worn much longer. The interest of the design is now on the front and back of the chasuble, which is slightly longer than the front. There is enormous scope for originality in the planning of the decoration, which will, if kept large and bold, 'tell up' dramatically when viewed from a distance. Often it is too small in detail. The chasuble is thought of in relation to the setting against which it will be seen. With the westward facing celebration the design interest is equally at the front and back.

Greater inventiveness can be achieved

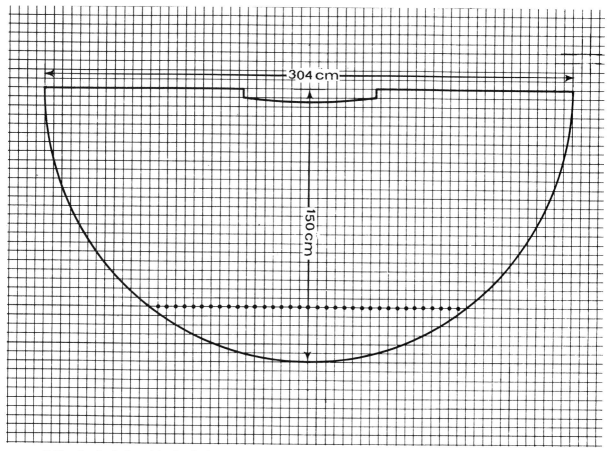

5 The Conical chasuble. Scale 1 square=5 cm

by evolving embroidered patterns based upon one or more suitable symbols incorporating smaller shapes and symbols; or the decoration can be a combination of more abstract forms, making use of contrasting textures in stitchery and fabric, and also colour. It is important to avoid meaningless abstraction which is out of key with the sacred purpose, as it seems empty and theatrical.

Seldom used now is the conventional Y-shaped orphrey, with its decoration centred in the vestment motif. The cross and pillar orphreys have a utilitarian origin, as the seams are covered, but a well-prepared seam does not require camouflaging. An interesting variation of the Y-shaped orphrey is to fill in the space with all-over decoration, making a yoke.

Certain limitations have to be respected when designing, for example the horizontal draping of the conical shape or the vertical folds of the chasuble of Gothic revival shape. Then, too, the slant of the shoulder prevents the horizontal arms from remaining at right angles to the upright in wear when the design is based on a large cross.

Measurements

These vary according to the shape, but generally chasubles are much longer than they were and fuller. The diagrams given must be adapted to the height of the wearer.

Shapes

The following suggestions are intended as a guide and can be adapted as necessary. The graphs are to scale; the dotted lines indicate a fold in the pattern. The length should be adjusted to the height of the wearer. The hemline of the same chasubles may be cut to a slight point at the front and back, if preferred.

Possible layouts are sketched (not to scale) for different widths of material. It will be noticed that the selvedge grain runs down the length of the back in each example. Considerations determining the positioning of seams in relation to the design make it impossible to indicate more than a few examples. It is seldom that a chasuble only would be cut out. To plan a complete layout for the whole set avoids wastage. For a figured material or one with a pile, allow extra for matching the patterning. The grain of pieces to be joined must correspond with that of the garment. (Either cut off or snip selvedges, as they tend to tighten up and cause puckering.)

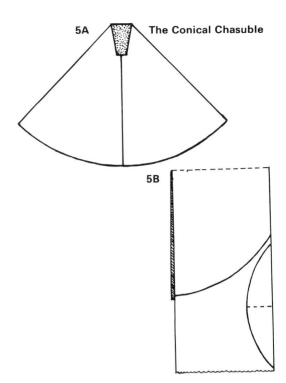

5A The Conical Chasuble

5B

**6 Modification of the Conical chasuble.
Scale 1 square=5 cm**

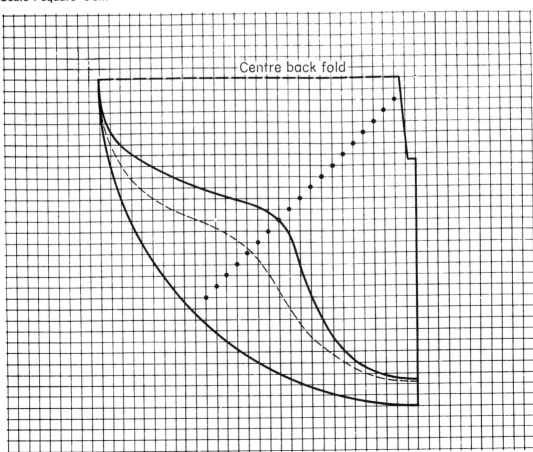

Centre back fold

The Conical Chasuble   This is a semi-circle, generally joined down the centre front (*5A*), but sometimes at the centre back. This chasuble is the authentic shaped *paenula* or conical chasuble. The dotted line shown on the graph indicates the join when 122 cm material is used. The layout (*5B*) shows the placing on the fabric.

In *figure 6* alternative shoulder lengths are given. From 150 cm or 122 cm wide fabric this chasuble can be cut in one piece. A Y-shaped orphrey covers the seams.

The Gothic Chasuble   This has a centre front and centre back seam (*7A*). When using 150 cm wide material it can be cut without other joins, the centre back goes to the selvedge; it is cut double. The sketched layout (*7B*) gives the arrangement for 122 cm material and the dotted line shows the position for a 92 cm width.

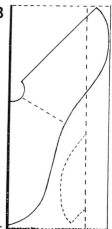

7B Layout for 122 cm fabric

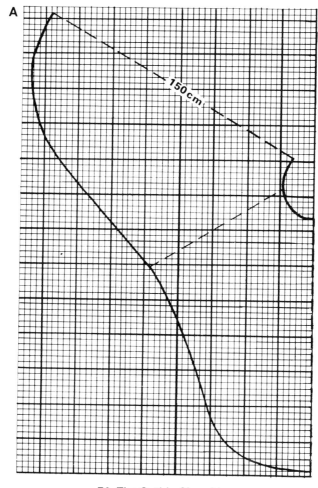

7A The Gothic Chasuble.
Scale 1 square=3.5 cm

The Gothic Revival Chasuble Although still popular this chasuble (8) looks much too skimpy, the shoulder seam and centre front and back are too short. It can be cut from 122 cm material without central seams. This can be seen from the layout (9). If there are Y-orphreys, the front and back must meet at the shoulder.

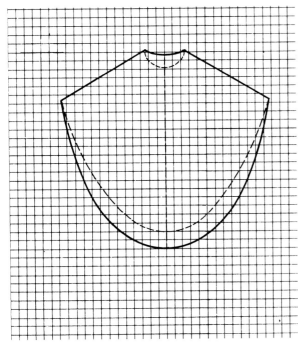

8 The Gothic Revival chasuble.
Scale 1 square=5 cm

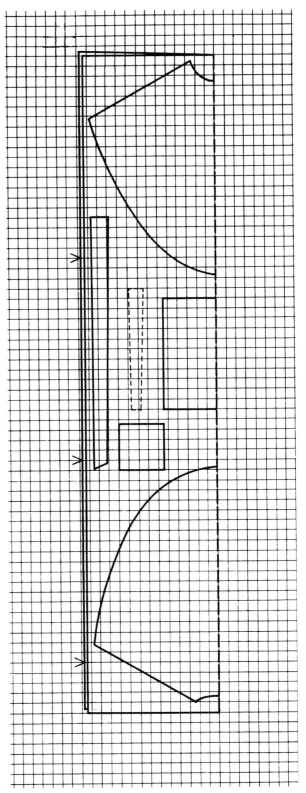

9 Layout for a Gothic Revival Eucharistic set.
Fabric 122 cm wide. Scale 1 square=5 cm

The 'Seamless' Garment This chasuble (*10*) falls in vertical folds and can only be cut from 150 cm wide material. The fold runs through the centre front and centre back.

The Roman or Latin Chasuble As can be seen from *figure 11A* the back shoulder can be extended and brought over to the front. The interlining would be dowlas, *Vilene*, tailors' or hair canvas. This form of chasuble is seldom made now.

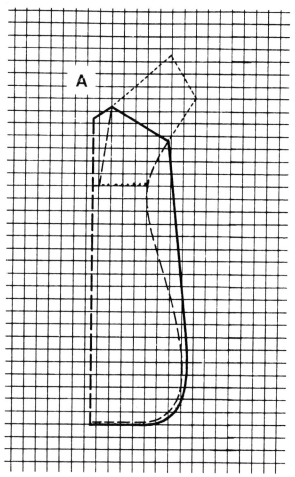

11A The Roman or Latin chasuble.
Scale 1 square=5 cm

10 The 'Seamless' Garment.
Scale 1 square=3.5 cm

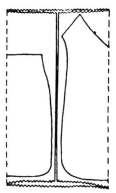

11B Layout for 150 cm fabric

Figure 12 shows the chasuble most generally worn. The length can be varied as can the length of the shoulder seam. It is usually necessary to have centre back and centre front seams. The smaller neckline is shown. There can be 7.5 cm openings on both shoulders, or one longer opening which is necessary when worn with the cassock alb. A decorative central neck opening is shown.

The layout (*13*) is planned for fabric 122 cm wide; the amount required would be about 5 m (the maniple is included if required).

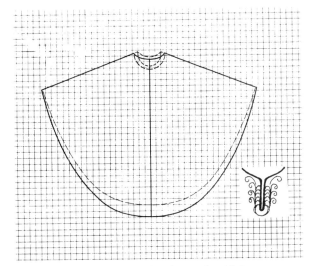

12 Modern chasuble, alternative higher neckline. Scale 1 square=5 cm

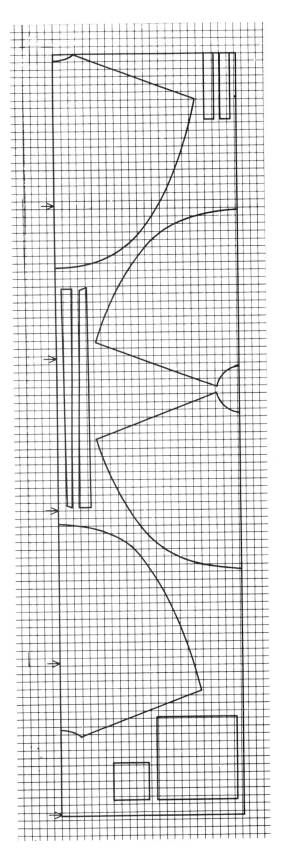

13 Layout for 122 cm wide fabric. Modern chasuble. Scale 1 square=5 cm

The chasuble (14), shows a fine line for the front, and a thick line for the back. This is the present-day type. The total length and shoulder seam can be adapted. It hangs in rich folds.

As for all the patterns, cut adding a seam and hem allowance, marking the stitching line.

For collar shown at A, put the centre back to the fold and cut double. Cut interlining.

Roll-collar, shown at B, is a straight strip cut on the true cross about 18 cm wide, the finished length equals that of the neck. It can be joined on the cross or straight through. If the ends of the join are left open in the centre front (C) a collar effect is obtained. The strip is folded along the centre. One way of attaching the edge to the neckline is to stitch the outer side, fold the roll over and hem the inner edge as shown at B. However this wide cross-cut strip is arranged when planning, it does increase the amount of material required.

A soft cross-cut interlining may be an advantage.

Some shapes of collar can be cut with a point at the back.

The chasuble is made up in the same way as the other types, except when a collar is added. When making A, having cut the collar pieces double, put the right sides together, lightly attach the interlining to the wrong side of the under-piece, stitch around the edge, turn out and press, having trimmed the outside turning. With the underside of the collar to the right side of the garment, match up the shoulder seam balance marks, stitch, and nick the turnings of the neckline. Bring the lining up to the stitch line and hem.

For an unlined chasuble a narrow cross-cut facing is used, as shown in the diagram.

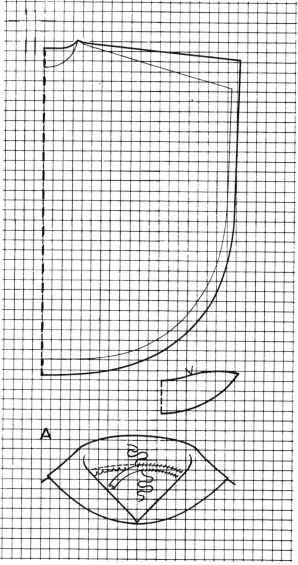

14 Modern chasuble with alternative collars.
Scale 1 square=4 cm

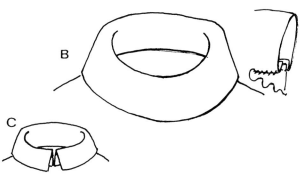

Making-up chasubles

Place the pattern on the fabric, tack, tailor-tack (if double) or chalk on the stitching line.

Cut, allowing for turnings and hems.

It is generally preferable to complete the embroidery before cutting out or making up any vestment. See *figures 127* and *128*.

When constructing an unlined chasuble, first neaten the back of any embroidery with a piece of thin silk. (The pattern lines would have been marked, and it would have been cut out.)

Where the seams are to be covered, they can be stitched on the right side of the garment. Stitch, and neaten other joins on the reverse side, the run and fell seam can be used.

On some materials it is possible to turn up a very narrow hem and invisibly stitch it. Or a narrow, cross-cut strip of facing is invisibly sewn on to the reverse side (*15D*).

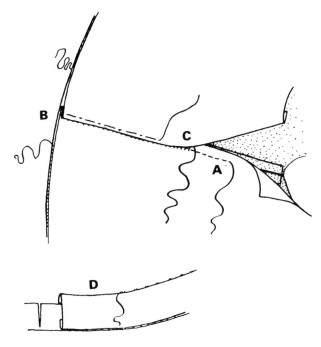

15A–E Locking the lining and the fabric together

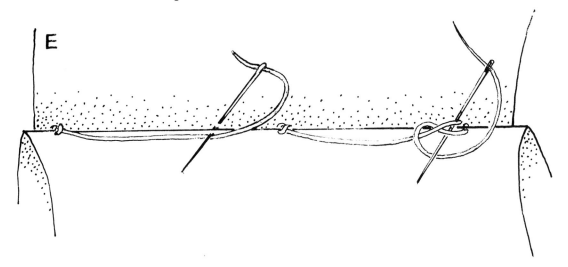

If, as another alternative, a straight braid is used to neaten the edge, it is seldom satisfactory.

The neck can be neatened with a cross-cut binding, or treated as for a lined chasuble (*16E,F*)

To make a lined chasuble with shoulder seams
1 Lay the front and back out flatly, face down. (If there is an interlining it should

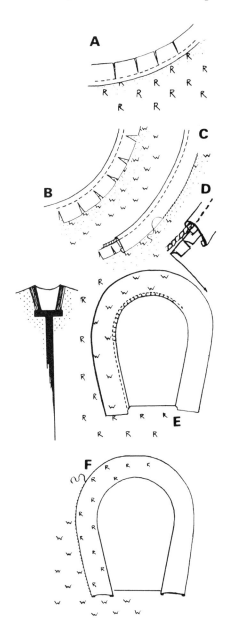

16(a)–(f) Necklines

be very light and soft; butter muslin for example. It is cut without turnings and very lightly attached at intervals, invisibly, to the silk.)

2 Turn up the hems, taking care not to stretch the parts on the cross; nick where necessary, catch stitch and press with the iron pointing inwards. (Sometimes it is sufficient to press it up without stitching.) The method shown for making-up a banner applies. See *figure 91*.

3 The lining, even for a Requiem chasuble, can be of a contrasting colour, but must not be stiff. Cut the lining pieces with good allowance for turnings. Mark the centre. The edges can be turned in and tacked, but this is not always necessary.

4 Then, with the front and the back of the chasuble lying face down, put the linings in position, matching up the centres. Fold back one half of the lining down the centre, and lock the edge of the fold to the inside of the fabric, invisibly, taking tiny stitches as shown at (*15E*) and very long ones between. (When making up copes it is necessary to do more rows of locking to prevent the lining dropping.) Then, pinning and tacking, smooth out from the centre and pin at intervals, keeping the pins all in the same direction; then put in a tack about 10 cm from the edge, and, if the lining turnings are prepared, the edge is put to the edge and slip-stitched. Some workers prefer to turn in the edges as they go, section by section, so that it is just inside the edge of the chasuble, pinning with the pins pointing inwards, then slip-stitching (*15B*). However this is done, if all lines of stitches start and finish about 5 cm short of the shoulder seam a much neater edge will result.

5 Place the right side of the front and back together, first folding back the linings, matching up the shoulder seam fitting lines, pin, tack and stitch the seams on the line, and press open. Then turn up two remaining sections of the hem,

catch-stitch and press (15).

6 Bring the back lining to lie over the seam and stitch it in self-colour along the seam line (15A). Fold in the remaining few centimetres of the outside edge and the shoulder turnings of the front lining (15C); put the fold to the seam line, tack and hem (15B), taking the stitches through the turnings but not allowing them to penetrate to the right side of the chasuble.

7 The neck should measure not less than 63.5 cm and up to 68.5 cm. A satisfactory, strong way of finishing the neck is with a piping. Prepare this as for the piping for the cusion and (16A,B,C,D) but taking the measurement of the neckline, and for an unlined chasuble allow one edge of the cross-cut materials to be wider than the other.

Stitch it on to the right side as shown in figure 16A, nicking both chasuble and piping edges. Turn it over on to the wrong side (16B). But for an unlined chasuble, turn in the centre width and hem it down invisibly (16C).

When the shape of the neck or the nature of the material calls for a shaped facing, this is cut in self-material, and is placed on the chasuble, right sides together then stitched; the edges are nicked, and it is then turned over on the wrong side (16F). Where, if the chasuble is unlined, the edges are neatened and caught down; if lined, it is lightly kept in place. Sometimes a shaped facing is put on the right side as decoration. Any neckline may be neatened with a cross-cut facing (16D), which would be mitred at the corners.

When the seams of the chasuble are central, the lining may be made up, and invisibly caught to the back of the fabric, as shown for the lining of the banner (91). Then the hems would be turned in and stitched. An alternative method is to stitch one lining piece to the back of the centre join, then hem on the other, in the way described for the chasuble with the shoulder seam.

To make-up the modern Roman and the fiddle back, join the back to the front; then cut the interlining, usually holland, dowlas or heavy *Vilene* cut to the size, and fold over the turnings, catch-stitching them, and hem in the lining. The processes are much the same as for the full chasuble, except for the addition of the interlining.

A quick method To make up a chasuble in this way is certainly NOT recommended, because the lining is apt to drop after a time, but it is very quick and sometimes expedient.

Having cut out chasuble and lining, cut a facing to fit the neckline using iron-on *Vilene* to the reverse side of the material. Stitch the shoulder seams of both, press open. Put the right sides of garment and lining together, stitch around the neckline, pave down turnings and snip, press open. Turn out the whole thing through the neckline, match up centres, catch the shoulder turnings together on the inside (as far as possible). Press up a narrow hem, bring the lining over the slip stitch.

An even quicker method, but even less to be recommended is to stitch round the whole of the outside, then turn out through the hole for the neck, press, and neaten the neckline.

THE STOLE

The stole forms a part of the Eucharistic set and is of symbolic significance. It conforms to the colour for the season. Although crosses so often formed the basis for the design, there can be greater latitude. The small cross at the back of the neck is still usual, and in the Roman rite, required. The embroiderer enjoys doing a stole, because the details of the technique can be appreciated at close range.

For the long narrow stole, about 7 to 8 cm wide, the decoration is generally at the ends or may extend throughout its length. Fringe is only added when it forms an integral part of the design.

The embroidery on the wide stole is towards the top, and is frequently asymmetrical, or the whole length may be decorated (*17*). As the wide stole is worn outside it is an important way of introducing colour.

The baptismal stole may be white or cream on one side and purple on the other. A deacon's stole is straight (as it is worn over one shoulder, it has an inconspicuous means of fastening).

The maniple is no longer required.

Most materials can be used, for example corded, ottoman or wild silk, Thai silk, fine wool or silk poult. Shantung or any fabric which will not slip can be used for the lining.

The Wide Stole

When the celebrant or president of the Eucharist started to enlist the assitance of the people, they tended to take and wear any stole which was the colour of the day. This, not having been intended for wearing outside, was unsuitable, so the new, wide stole, emerged to be worn over the cassock alb. They vary in width from 11 to 20 cm and can fall to within 15 cm of the ground. Broad stoles are often reversible and afford the embroiderer unlimited scope. Many materials can be used, including the handsome wide braids woven for the purpose. Stoles conform to the liturgical colours.

17 Stole designed by the Rev Leonard Childs for Derby Cathedral

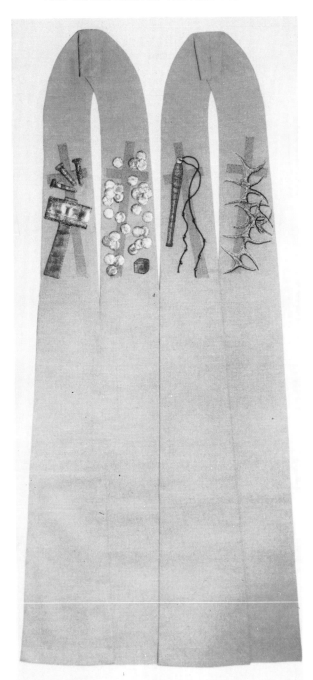

18 Passion Tide stole (wide) by Joyce Williams

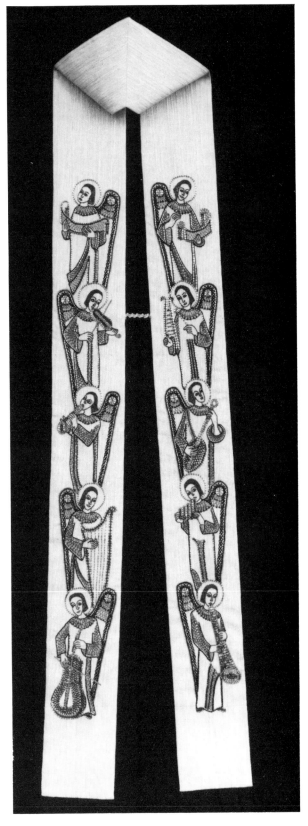

19(a) Stole, by Wefers, Cologne, West Germany

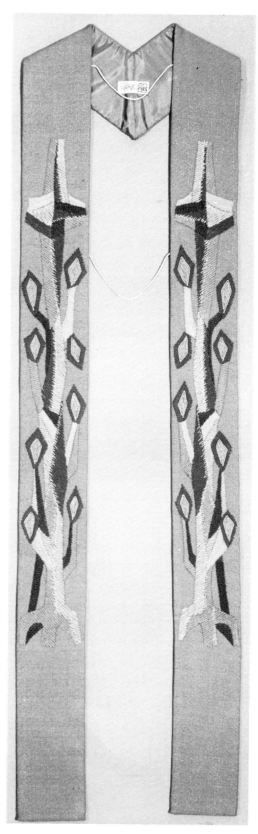

19(b) Detail

20(a) The broad stole, by Düster, Cologne, West Germany. Made from a cotton mixture, green, and worked with synthetic threads and synthetic gold cord. It shows the mitred point at the back join

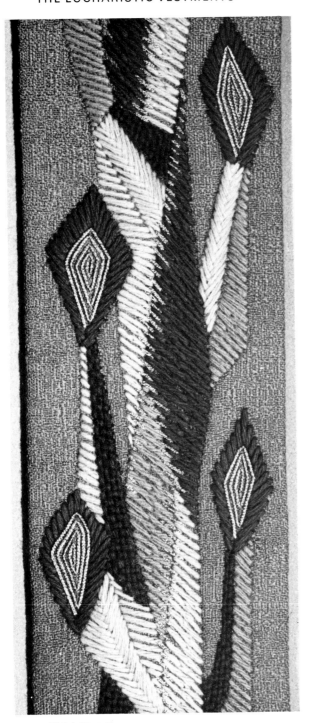

20(b) Detail

There are several ways of dealing with the neck, the simplest being the mitred join (*21B*) or it can be curved at the neckline as shown in *figure 21A,C*. This stole can be made longer.

Measurements

The Eucharistic stole is generally longer than the pastoral or preaching stole, and it shows below the chasuble. Length 2.7 m width at the base 7 to 9 cm; it can narrow to 5 to 6.5 cm at the neck.

Stoles are usually long and narrow, and can be a strip of uniform width, without a centre back seam.

Method for the long straight stole

Draft the pattern (*21E*). Adapt the length to the height of the wearer. Place on the fabric, preferably with the grain remaining downwards.

Mark round the stitching line.

Cut, leaving turnings.

Next prepare to do the embroidery.

Trace on the design.

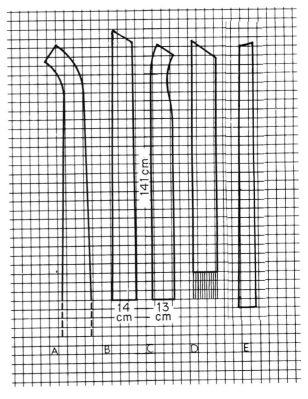

21 Stoles. Scale 1 square=5 cm

Frame up the backing (refer to the section on embroidery) and see *figure 22A*.

Stitch the stole pieces in position, roll the remaining length over something soft.

Work the embroidery. See *figure 22A*.

Do the centre join, put it over the backing and work the small cross. Or it can be worked in the hand after the stole has been removed from the frame.

Take the embroidery out of the frame, and cut the backing away, partially or it is generally better to cut close to the embroidery, or the backing can be cut along the pattern line.

Cut two pieces of interlining (dowlas, holland or *Vilene*) a fraction inside the pattern line, except at the centre back where each is extended by about 5 cm.

Put the stole out flat, face down.

Take the pieces of interlining, and smoothing upwards from the ends allow them to overlap at the neck, pin and tack; zigzag tack the interlining (*22C*).

Re-shape by cutting interlining and the turnings at the neck into a slight curve. Snip concave and clip convex turnings (*22D*). If embroidered in the hand, the centre back cross can be worked now.

Fold the turnings of the stole over the interlining, catch stitch or herringbone, working from each end upwards to the centre back so that (should any adjustment become necessary, it can be done by moving the overlapped interlining.) This can be seen at the foot of *figure 22E*.

Press the turning on the wrong side.

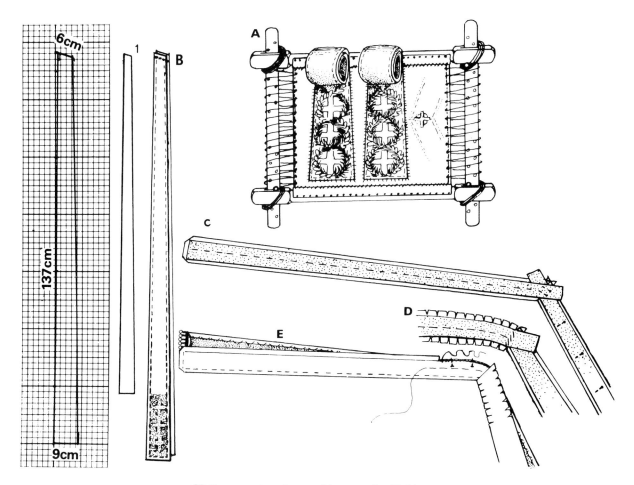

22 Frame set up for working a stole. Making-up stoles

THE EUCHARISTIC VESTMENTS

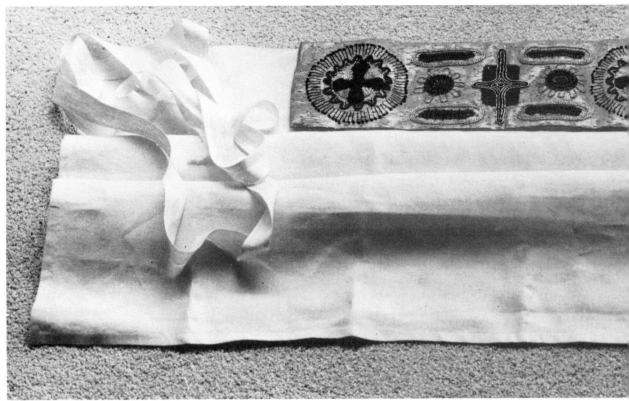

23 Amice, with apparel, by Pam Waterworth

Cut two lining pieces, allowing turnings. Stitch the centre back seam at exactly the same angle as the one on the front side of the stole (*22E*). Press open.

Put the centre back lining seam over the centre back join of the stole. Pin.

Smooth out the lining towards the bottom, and, working towards the bottom, pin and tack the lining in place, down the middle.

Starting from the centre back fold in the turnings a fraction inside the fitting line, snipping at the inner curve and clipping at the outer curve of the neck, tack (either as shown in the diagram, or through the interlining). When a contrasting colour is used for the lining the fold should exactly coincide with the edge, yet not show from the right side. Next, slip-stitch or invisibly hem, starting from the centre back (*22E*).

The heading of a fringe (if used) would be stitched to the wrong side of the front of the stole, and the lining hemmed over it.

The processes of making-up for the different stoles follow in much the same way.

If preferred adhesives prepared for using on fabrics can replace catch stitching the turning to the back of the interlining.

The Amice

This is a neck cloth worn under the alb, it is a rectangle of white linen, tied with tapes (*24*). The fabric apparel, plain or with embroidery is of the liturgical colour of the day.

Conventionally a small cross is worked in the centre about 4 cm in from the edge, or a band of embroidery worked in washable threads. One side is turned down over the chasuble.

The amice measures 92 cm × 61 cm plus turnings for hems.

The apparel measures 51 cm × 8 cm and is made of the material of the set, whether plain or embroidered it is interlined and lined, it is then tacked into place on the

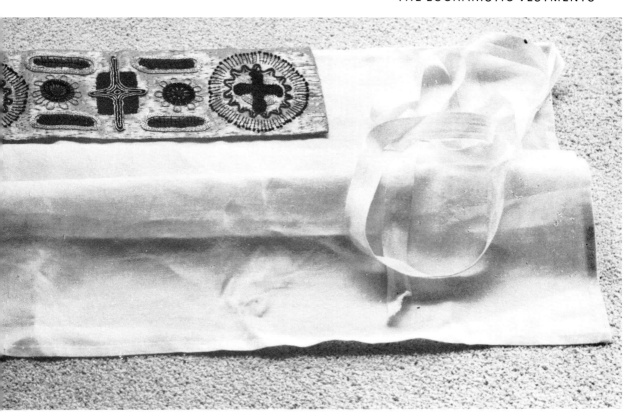

amice, to be removed when necessary.

A narrow hem is stitched round the rectangle and the tapes about 150 cm long, are attached on the short sides, about 8 cm in from the long edge, as this turns over to form a collar. When the cassock alb is worn the amice is unnecessary.

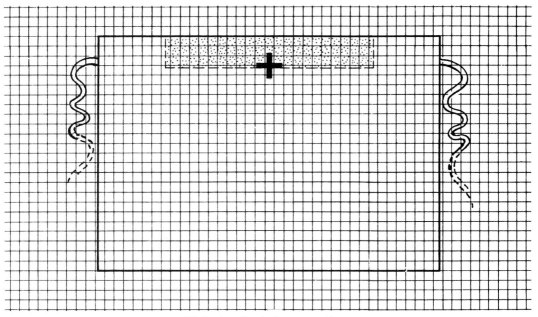

24 Amice. Scale 1 square=5 cm

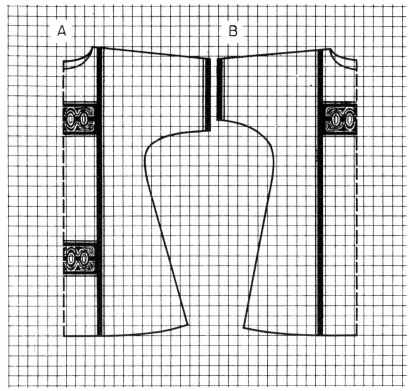

25 Dalmatic and Tunicle, with shoulder seam.
Can be made longer and without decoration.
Scale 1 square=5 cm

DALMATIC AND TUNICLE

Worn by the deacon or gospeller and sub-deacon or epistoler respectively. These vestments are gradually being replaced by the cassock alb worn with the wide stole. The dalmatic, which has wide sleeves sometimes with a cuff, and the tunicle with longer narrower sleeves, are a part of the whole High Mass or Eucharistic set of vestments and are made from the same material. Both can be longer than suggested in the diagrams. The shorter, stiffer shapes, which were almost entirely open at the sides are seldom made now.

If the clavi on the back and front take the form of bands of colour or are of embroidered decoration, these should tie in with the set as a whole, so also should the two apparels, back and front, on the dalmatic and the one on the tunicle, which are not now always added.

Measurements

The centre back length varies from 114 to 140 cm and the shoulder seam length about 55 cm. Add to this for the width of the dalmatic cuff if included.

For the tunicle the sleeve is a little longer and narrower.

Figure 25A shows a dalmatic with a shoulder seam, and a seam down the line of the clavi. At *25B* the pattern for a tunicle with its narrower sleeves (which may be made longer) is given.

The dalmatic and tunicle are made in much the same way as a chasuble, except that the clavi seams and decoration are completed first. It is important to nick the turnings of the underarm curves and advisable to catch the reverse side of the lining seams to the reverse side of the garment seams where possible.

It will be seen in *figure 26A* that there is a fold at the shoulder and an inset gusset at the underarm. Shaping may be introduced into the clavi seams. Remember that this pattern cannot be used with an up-and-down fabric design. The sleeve must be made a little longer and narrower for the tunicle.

The little square gusset is stitched into one side first, then the seams are done and the other edges of the gusset. Otherwise it is similar to making a chasuble.

The adaptation for an inverted pleat

The adaptation of the pattern for an inverted pleat is shown in *figure 26B*. Both edges of the clavi seam are extended about 8 cm, at about 23 cm down from the shoulder.

When making-up it is generally prefer-

able to deal with the pleat whilst the garment is spread out flatly. First, join together the top 23 cm of the seam, press open and do the centre seam of the pleat (*26C*) and arrange the inverted pleat. Then put together the remainder of the garment.

Next make the lining, it may be easier if the top 23 cm (46 cm) of the seam is left open, until the rest of the lining has been fixed. This section of the seam can then be stitched by hand. The top of the pleat is neatened with a narrow cross-cut strip of lining material.

The lining is then stitched to the neck, sleeves and hem, as for a chasuble. The side seams can be left open at the bottom if preferred.

With experience, other ways will be

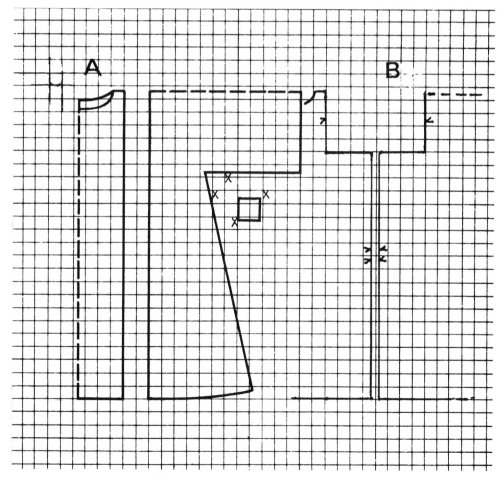

26 A, B Dalmatic with adaptation.
Scale 1 square=5 cm

found for dealing with the inverted pleat. See *figure 26D*.

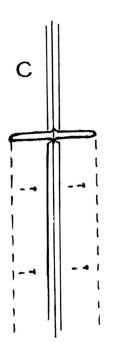

THE HUMERAL VEIL

This is worn round the priest's shoulders at certain parts of the Mass and at Benediction. A cross or suitable emblem is frequently, but not necessarily, worked in the centre. It is important that any decoration should not be stiff or heavy. The humeral veil matches the Eucharistic or Benediction set.

Material
Generally the same as that used for the whole set, provided that it drapes well and is not stiff. Or it can be made of a very light material.

Measurements
About 3 m or less long × 61 to 76 cm wide.

Method
When unlined the hems are neatly finished on the reverse side; the fastening (*27A*), either a little chain with hook, or narrow

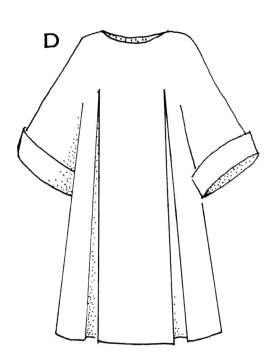

26 C, D Dalmatic, with inverted pleats

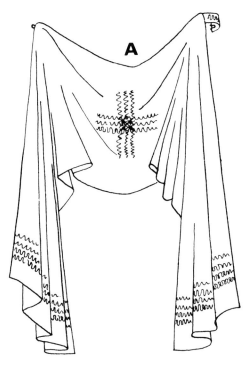

27 A, B The Humeral veil

strip with hook and eye, is attached about 61 cm apart (the same position as the morse on the cope). There can be a decorative treatment around the edges of the veil.

A light, soft material such as Jap silk is suitable for a lining; sometimes flat pockets made from lining material are stitched in place across the ends (or across two corners) on the reverse side of the veil (27B).

The turnings of the long, then the short, sides are pressed down, the fastening made and attached, then the edges of the lining turned in, pressed, then pinned, keeping the pins at right angles to the edge. (If there are pockets these would have been made and pinned in position.) The whole veil would then be slip-stitched or hemmed right round.

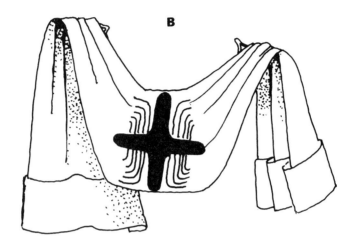

THE BURSE

The folded corporal (or corporals) are kept in the burse. When the vessels are compacted, the burse is placed on top of the chalice veil. When not in use, it generally stands upon the altar with the hinge uppermost. More often in the Roman Catholic Church it has the gussets at the sides and it stands on its side (29H).

Design
The burse is an interesting object to design as there is plenty of scope for experimentation in both subject and technique. Traditionally a cross formed the basis of the design as it can be seen from any angle. If there is an 'up and down' to the design, the practice followed in the particular church must be ascertained as it does not always

stand with the hinge to the top. The burse and veil go together. They usually form a part of the full Eucharistic set and may be made in each of the liturgical colours if desired by the authorities of the church for which they are made.

Measurements
Two stiffened squares of 20 to 25 cm, usually 23 cm.

Material
Usually matches the set of vestments, almost any fabric is suitable if not too thick, as it has to be cleaned anyway. White linen must be used for the lining.

Method 1
Have four 23 cm squares of cardboard cut, or they can be purchased already prepared.

28 Burse and Veil designed by Katarin Privett, worked by Pam Waterworth

(The two for the lining may be thinner.) Mark the centres each way.

1 Tack round the front and back squares on the fabric, cut, leaving about 2.5 cm turnings except on one side of the back where a 5 cm turning should be left. Do not cut away the backing from the embroidery as it helps to lessen the rub upon the material at the edges.

2 Place the embroidery face down, put the board in position, matching up the centres, then bend over the edge of the fabric, cut across for the corners and pin all round, top and bottom first, then the sides. Lace across the back with strong thread downwards first then across (29A). Sticking is quicker, but a poor substitute as it is not possible to get the material really taut.

3 The two squares for the lining are covered in the same way, using washed white linen.

4 These can be oversewn along one edge. (But a better hinge is produced by making a narrow fold of linen less than 6 mm

wide and 23 cm long and oversewn first to one side of the front then to one side of the back (29B) on the wrong side of each. Usually unnecessary.)

5 For the back of the burse, set the board in position for lacing, but stitch or stick to the board the side opposite that with the 5 cm turning; this is left loose at this stage. Then the other side can be laced across or stuck (29C).

6 Close the lining, lace the embroidered square on the front, and when there is a top and bottom to the design bear in mind that the burse generally stands with the hinge uppermost. Next, put the back square on the other side with the 5 cm turning on top. Hold the four together with the left hand and with the right tuck the turning down behind the front square, and pin (29D). Then invisibly slip-stitch along; this forms the hinge (29D) and the burse should close flatly; if it does not, let out the turning a little before stitching.

7 Pin and oversew the lining and the right sides together all round (29E). It is seldom that gussets are specifically required now, but should this be so they are made separately and lined (29H), being 2.5 cm

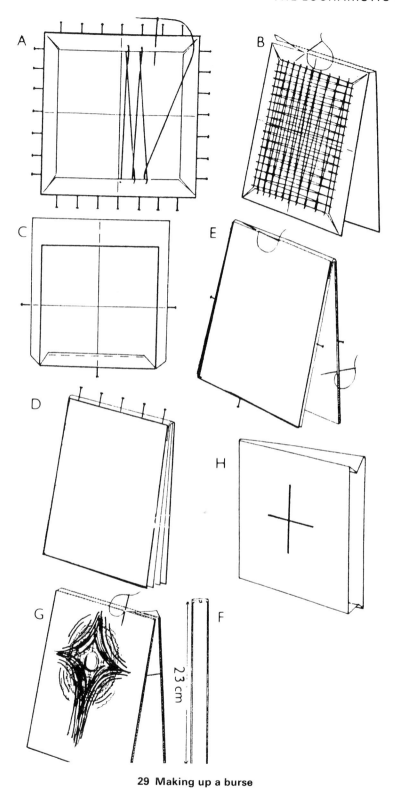

29 Making up a burse

30 Burse 'The Tree of Life' worked by Lieselotte Schober for Wefers of Cologne

wide at the top and tapering, pinned and oversewn around the edge, or it may be a 3 cm wide and 7.6 cm long (finished) strip material folded into a pleat; either way the edges are oversewn to the sides of the burse at the gusset end.

8 Some sort of neatening may be unavoidable. This should be carefully thought out so that it may be in keeping with the general scheme. An ordinary cord is too clumsy.

9 A little bar can be worked or small piece of narrow elastic can be stitched to the sides instead of a gusset.

Method 2

Complete all four squares as before (excluding the one with the 5 cm turnings). Take the front and its lining, putting them together, oversew round the outside; do the same with the back.

Make and line with linen a strip 9.5 cm wide and 23 cm long (*29F*), put one side to the top edge of the front of the burse, and the other to the top of the back and oversew. The edges of each square will, of course, have to be neatened all round (*29G*).

Method 3

The preparation is again the same as *method 2* except for the hinge. Instead of the strip of material little bars are worked across at intervals of about 5 cm to join the front and back together and form a hinge. This is very simple, but does not look as good as either of the other methods when finished.

THE CHALICE VEIL
OR
THE SILK VEIL

The veil covers the compacted chalice, the pall and the paten, both before and after use for the consecration. One side is turned back with the lining showing to allow the priest's hands to reach the chalice (*31A*).

Design

Similar to that for the burse, generally a cross in the centre of one side. There is no reason for not extending some embroidery around the other sides provided that it does not prevent the veil from falling softly; it must not make the veil heavy. For a time the burse rests on top of the veil which is another reason for having no embroidery in the middle. It will be seen from the diagram that figures or birds, for example, if included, should be designed to stand the right way up when the veil is in position.

Measurements

A square of 51–61 cm, but usually for the Church of England it is 54 or 56 cm square.

The size depends upon the height of the chalice.

Material

Matches or combines with the burse, and is frequently a part of the Eucharistic set. The fabric must fall in soft folds, for example, light grosgrain. (See the section devoted to fabrics page 12.) If an interlining is used it should be something soft such as butter muslin. The lining, too, is soft, usually silk and can be coloured. Shantung is excellent, or a good quality sateen or suran, if not shiny.

Method

Cut the backing away close to the embroidery. Allow about 2 cm turnings all round, fold these over, cutting across at the corners and very lightly catch-stitch to the back of the fabric, taking care that no stitches penetrate right through. (Should the lining be at all 'floppy', it is necessary to catch it with stitches to the back of the fabric at widely spaced intervals.) Then the edges are turned in and it is slip stitched round the outside (*31B*).

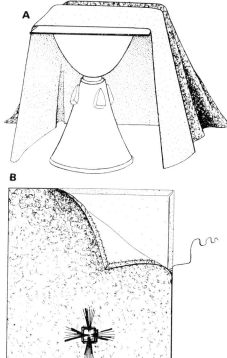

31 The Veil

32 Canterbury Cope, green, designed by Beryl
Dean

THE COPE

The earliest forms of cope were full and graceful with shaping at the shoulders, and narrow orphreys, which fell straight in front without overlapping. The hood was a genuine one, and was therefore hung from the top edge of the orphrey. From all aspects, appearance, and comfort in wearing, this shape is preferable, and there is a return to it (*33*).

In Italy in the seventeenth century the cope suffered great degradation. It became semicircular, with a wide stiff orphrey along the straight edge, which sometimes exceeded 20 cm in width; and in this form rises almost above the head at the back.

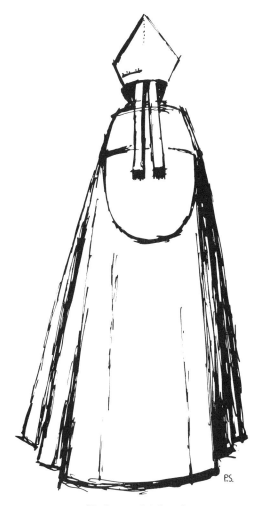

34 Cope with hood

33 Cope with hood

Also the bottom points in front are apt to overlap in wear. The hood became a large flat tab, attached below the orphrey and falling almost to the knees. In this form it was copied in England in the nineteenth century (*34*) – but generally with the hood attached to the upper edge of the orphrey.

Material

The cope may or may not conform to the liturgical colours. The fabric should hang well and be fairly heavy (if too weighty, however, it is uncomfortable). A very loose weave will stretch and drop after time, causing the hemline to become uneven. Many hand-woven and furnishing fabrics are interesting, although the joins in

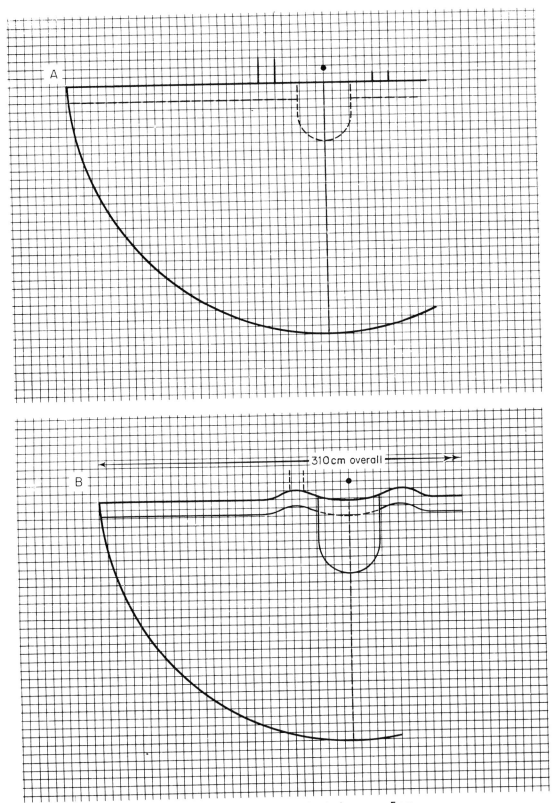

35 A, B Patterns of copes. Scale 1 square=5 cm

unlined copes present a problem. The lining should be firm and not too thin or 'slippery'.

Measurements

The average length down the centre back is 150 cm and the total along the straight edge is 3 to 3.8 m; the orphrey is about 11 cm wide, and the hood varies.

A cope planned as more than a semicircle hangs in deeper, richer folds. *Figure 35A,B,C* gives patterns of flat copes which are more simple to make than fitted copes. Try out the pattern in any piece of fabric.

Method

The layout must vary with the width of fabric and the patterning on it (*36*). With a 156 cm material it may have one join down the centre back, or to avoid a seam the selvedge can run parallel with the long side, and, if the orphrey is attached as an extension, the shaping is introduced without deducting from the centre back length. But this and any similar arrangement means that the centre back may not hang so well, as it is on the wrong way of the material. For narrower materials this is not recommended as a seam crosses the back. Another layout for any width of fabric is arrived at by putting the centre of the pattern to the centre fold (grain running down) of the material, and joining a width to either side (*37*); for a figured material this is preferable. When calculating the total amount allow extra for matching up the design.

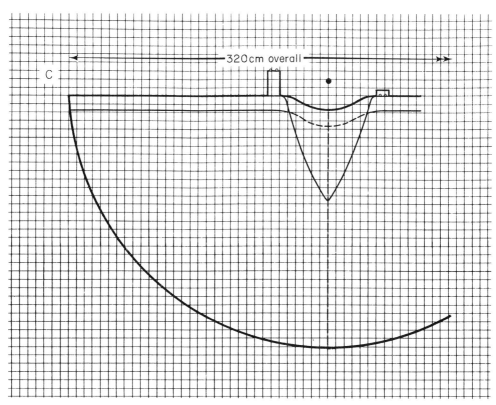

35 C Cope with hood. Scale 1 square=5 cm

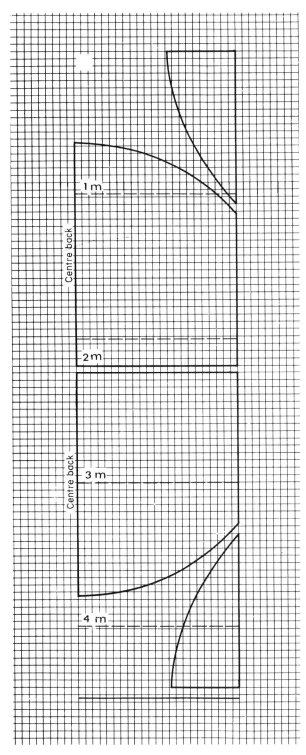

36 Cope. Layout for 122 cm material. Scale 1 square=5 cm

The embroidery

This can be worked either before or after the seams have been stitched. The instructions given for framing-up the chasuble, altar frontal and stole would apply. The orphrey may be worked on a long frame with short sides. The hood would be worked on a smaller frame. The cowl hood can either be embroidered on the inside or the outer side or both; the latter would necessitate framing-up both pieces of material.

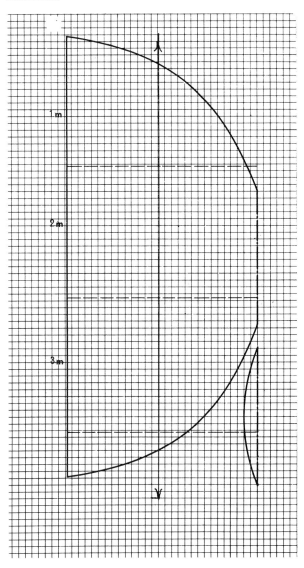

37 Cope. Layout for 150 cm wide material. Scale 1 square=5 cm

HOODS

For a flat hood (381,2) complete the embroidery. Cut, allowing turnings, fold these over the interlining, except for the top edge. Neaten the underside with a lining.

For a cowl hood (383) put the pattern upon two thicknesses of material, mark the centres, and snip *(39A)*. Fold each piece, right sides facing, stitch along the base line *(39B)* or each, press the seams open. Then with the right sides together fit one piece inside the other and stitch round the outside *(39C)*. Turn through to the right side (through the open top edge); press the seam flatly. Arrange it into folds, making pleats at either side; stitch along the top edge *(39D)*.

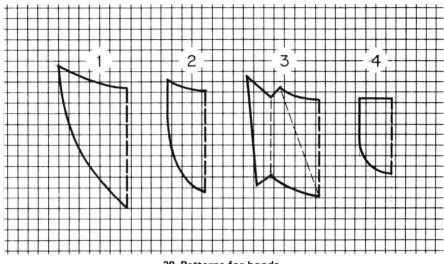

38 Patterns for hoods.
Scale 1 square = 5 cm

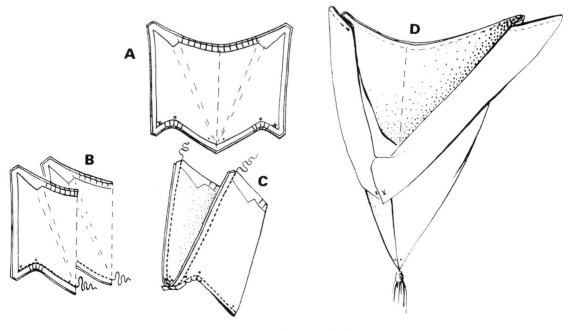

39 Making the cowl hood

Construction

Generally it is preferable to place the completed hood to the uncut and unfinished edge of the orphrey, so that the two can be shaped together; they then correspond. One method for attaching the hoods is shown in *figure 40*. The orphrey is usually made up in the same way as the stole, allowing for the shaping when necessary. The interlining may be holland or *Vilene*. Do not, however, put the lining in at this stage.

1 Join the seams of the cope; if the selvedge is not cut off then nip at intervals. Press open. For an unlined cope the inside must be neatened as invisibly as possible.

2 If the hood is to be attached to the underside of the orphrey, put the centre to the centre of the top of the cope, and stitch. (If it is to be detachable, using buttons, hooks or *Velcro*, this does not apply.)

3 Spread the cope out flat, put the orphrey in position, keeping the pins at right angles to the edge-tack, and stitch. Conventionally, this is covered with a braid, but this is not always an advantage.

4 Place the top edge of the completed hood to the top of the orphrey, stitch, neaten with a narrow braid, or turn the edge of the hood over on to the wrong side of the orphrey and catch-stitch or herringbone. Or do not cut or finish the neck shaping of the cope or orphrey. Pin the hood in position, and cut the two together so that the shaping corresponds on both. Snip the turnings. Stitch, fold the turnings over and herringbone or catch-stitch (*40*).

5 Make the morse; stitch two or three large hooks to it. The eyes are sewn to a small rectangle of fabric; both have an interlining and both are attached to the edge.

6 For an unlined cope, line the orphrey as for a stole, which neatens the joining of the cope and orphrey.

7 Allow the cope to hang for a time

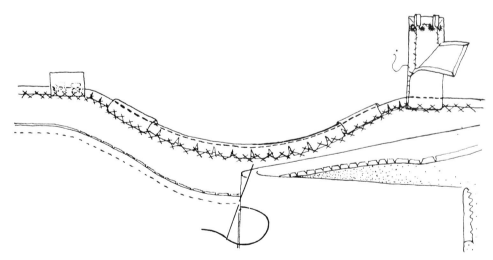

40 Sewing in the lining

before correcting the hemline.

For an *unlined* cope, a narrow hem may be turned up; this necessitates darting at intervals. It is more satisfactory to face the hem up with a cross-cut facing. (See the treatment of chasuble hems page 20.) Or it can be neatened with a braid or in some decorative way.

For a *lined* cope spread the cope out flat, face down. If an interlining should be an advantage, use some soft fabric such as muslin or flat domette; this is cut to the exact size, and lightly and invisibly caught at intervals to the back of the cope.

Then turn the hem over this (about 2 to 2.5 cm would have been allowed). Press up and very lightly catch-stitch.

8 Cut out the lining, allowing about 2 cm all round; the grain of the material must correspond with that of the garment. Stitch and press seams.

Then, with the centre back line over the centre of the cope, smooth outwards, pinning with the pins horizontally, and tack.

Usually the lining needs to be lightly caught to the back of the cope. This can be done either by folding it back only at the seams of the cope and stitching it invisibly through, or by folding it back at about 28 cm intervals and invisibly catching, or locking it to the fabric (taking care not to penetrate to the front) (*40*). Then the lining is moved over and a fresh fold is caught down; when one side is finished, work outwards from the centre to the other side. This whole process can be done horizontally instead of vertically.

9 Put a tack through to keep the materials together, about 8 cm from the edge, having smoothed out the lining.

10 Most workers prefer to turn in the hem of the lining as they go, pinning it with pins at right angles to the hem, then tacking, and hemming or slip-stitching the edges together, or with the lining a little way inside.

COPE (*figure 41*)

This cope hangs in rich folds and moves well, it is comforable to wear as it fits at the shoulders, but experience is required when attempting to make it. The shape of the cope makes it suitable for embroidery on the back and front panels (which are cut as rectangles for framing-up and cut out to shape when completed). There is no orphrey as the hood forms a collar at the front. The pattern fits a wearer of average size and height. When drawing out the pattern from the diagram (*41*) the size can be slightly increased by adding 2.5 to 5 cm at the centre back, it is necessary to adjust the front and back neckline and shoulder line.

It is advisable to cut (allowing good turnings) the pattern preferably in muslin, marking the stitching lines. Tack together the pattern pieces, matching up the balance marks. When fitting on to the wearer, tether the centre back, make any necessary alterations to seam lines and length (the front should be slightly shorter).

Having selected a suitable fabric (neither too heavy nor too light) place the pattern pieces with the centres down the grain of the material. Check that the pile or woven design runs in the same direction throughout.

Mark the stitching line and balance marks. Cut, allowing good turnings and leaving plenty at the hemline in case a future wearer is taller.

Using *Vilene*, tailors' canvas, hair canvas or dowlas (duck) as an interlining for the front edges, cut this about 10 cm wide, continue it round the neck making this part narrower. Attach this invisibly to the reverse side of the fabric. No turnings on interlining.

Put running stitches from A to B at the top of the side panel, pull this up very slightly (not more than 4 cm).

Stitch the shoulder seam, press open.

Put the shoulder balance mark (arrow) to the shoulder seam (right sides facing)

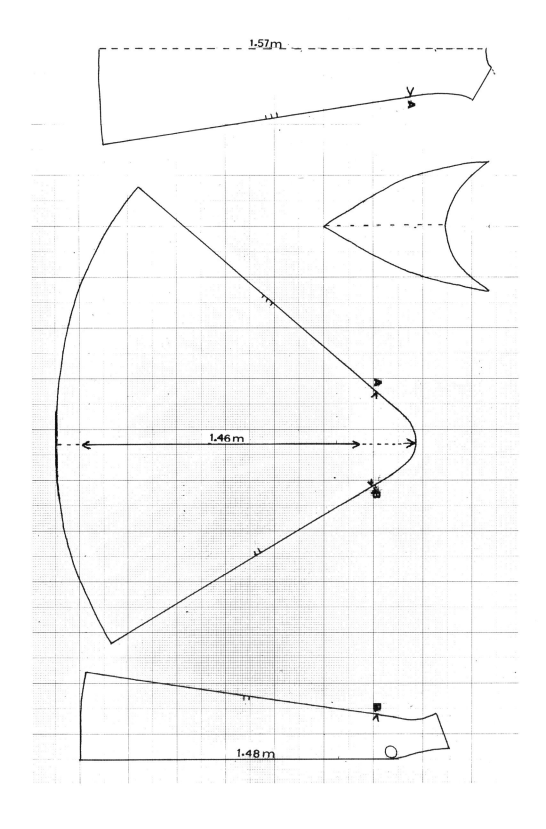

keeping the side panel over the body of the cope, in the same way as for putting in a sleeve. Pin, keeping the pins at right angles to the seam. Match up balance marks and pin remainder of the seams, tack, stitch, press open. (Use the special board for pressing velvet.)

Turn up the hem, lightly press (putting dry cloth between garment and hem) loosely catch-stitch if necessary.

Fold the front turnings over the interlining and catch-stitch. (A decorative piping gives a firmer edge.)

Cut and make-up the lining in the same way, except for hem and edges.

Spread out the cope as flat as possible on a large table, right side down.

With the reverse sides together, put the lining in position.

Starting from the centre back, put the back seams together (the rest of the lining has to be folded out of the way). Lightly catch the lining seam to the cope seam.

Next, fold out the remainder of the side panel lining, and fix one seam over the other, smooth out, starting at the shoulder and matching up the balance marks on both the lining and the cope, stitch using tiny stitches, these can be about 4 cm apart but must not penetrate to the right side, and should be quite loose).

Stitch around the neckline and nick the turnings at intervals.

Fold in the turnings all round the edges of the cope and invisibly slip-stitch or hem.

◀ 41 Cope. Add hem and seam allowance when cutting. Scale 1 square=1 cm

THE HOOD

If the width of the cope has been extended at the centre back, a similar modification must be made to the hood.

The embroidery on the hood will have been completed.

When cutting out leave plenty of turning at the neckline.

Place the interlining (no turnings) over the reverse side of the hood, turn over the edges, catch-stitch and line.

Nick the turnings at the neckline.

Place the centre of the hood to the centre of the cope, tack. At this stage it must be fitted on the wearer, as adjustments may well be needed. Mark the position for the morse.

When corrected, stitch the hood to the cope, trim the turnings. Neaten with a narrow band of cross-cut material. (This is the most straightforward method.)

It is intended that there should be a metal clasp morse, which should be strongly sewn in place. The position is suggested by a circle on the diagram.

THE CANTERBURY COPE
(figure 42)

The dotted line shown on the pattern for the Canterbury cope (32) was made from the original 'toile'. It will be seen that this pattern can be adapted from cope, figure 41, which is to scale.

The side seam allows for extra shaping. More width across the chest and shoulders can be obtained by raising the side pieces, for this reason additional length needs to be allowed.

When the cope has been cut (with turnings), preferably in muslin or calico, and tacked up, it is essential to fit it on the wearer, with the turnings outside, so that the shaping at the shoulders can be corrected.

The process of making both copes is similar, except that there is no need for the easing at the shoulder of this cope, and the

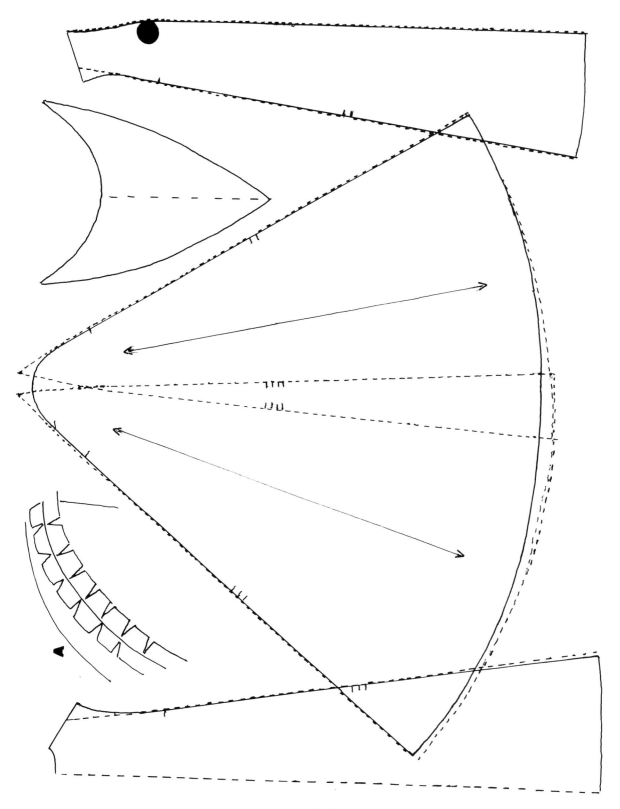

1.57m

additional side seam is stitched from the neck through to the hemline. This is pressed open and will probably require nicking at the shoulder (*A*).

THE MITRE

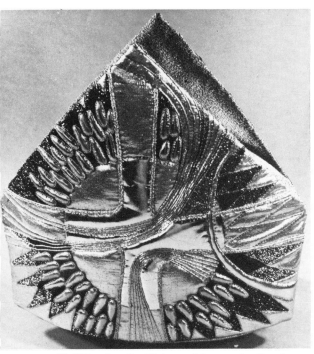

43 Mitre for the Bishop of Jarrow by Beryl Dean

Mitres are worn by archbishops and bishops. There are slight variations of shape, several different methods of construction, and many possible forms of decoration. The tall, wide, mitre of Baroque origin is now considered decadent.

Design

The conventional, contrasting, central orphrey and headband, although serving to hide the joins, have many more interesting alternatives. The design should befit the purpose intended for each mitre; some are simple, some elaborate.

42 Cope. Pattern for the Canterbury Cope

Material

This generally matches or goes with the cope. The colour need not conform to the liturgical colours. From cloth of gold to linen. Any fabric which is not too thick can be used.

Measurements

An average head measurement is 58 to 59 cm, but this varies individually.

44 Mitre for the Bishop of Lewes by Beryl Dean

Method 1

For a simple shape, with the point at 45 degrees. Complete the embroidery.

Cut a rectangle of fabric 46 cm × 29.30 cm allowing 2 cm turnings extra (*45A*). Mark the dotted lines with tacks, fold in half across, right sides together. Stitch and press open the centre front and back seams. (It may be necessary to finish by hand some of the embroidery which crosses over the join.) Turn out to the right side (*45B*).

Next, with the centre front over the centre back, fold for the sides 7.5 cm up, marked with an arrow (*45B*).

Then press in folds from the arrows to the points marked with crosses (*45C*). These lines can be defined by sewing cords or couching threads along them.

The stiffening can be sparterie, canvas or

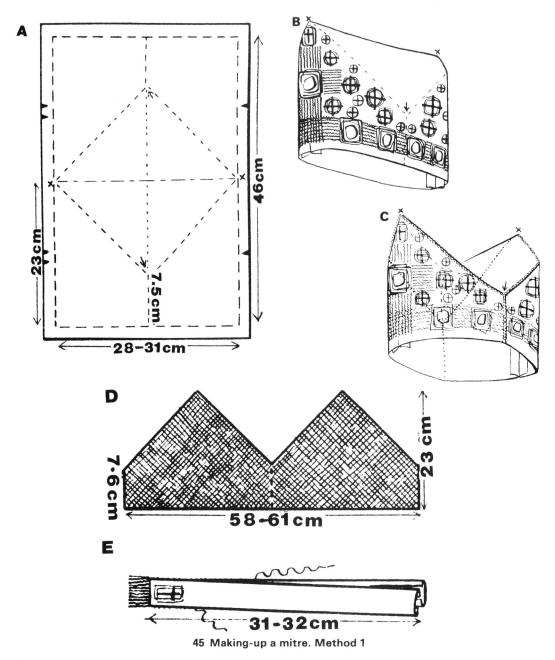

45 Making-up a mitre. Method 1

buckram. Cut the stiffening, without turnings (*45D*). If the join (or joins) at the side is to be overlapped allow turnings.

This stiffening should be covered with a thin fabric on both sides; cut, allowing turnings all round. For the outside fold the turnings over, catch-stitch. Press down the turnings of the second piece of lining, hem or slip-stitch around the edges, but leave the headline open.

Put the stiffening inside the mitre, pushing the points right up and catching them in place with a stitch. Fold the turnings of the mitre over the headline of the stiffening (*46F*). Make and attach the lappets to the centre back (*45E*). Catch-stitch or herringbone the turning to the headline of the inside of the stiffenings. Then neaten this by covering it with the unattached edge of the inside lining (*46F*). (This would have been pinned back out of the way.) Hem or slip-stitch round the hemline. Fold across the soft top of the mitre so that it lies flat (*46G*).

Method 2

Here, the front and back are each completed, then joined at the sides, with gusset added; this allows for variations of shape. Contrasting colours can be introduced, and the measurements varied.

Having finished the embroidery, cut, leaving turnings all round each piece (*46H*), also the gusset. Cut out the two pieces of stiffening without turnings (*46I*).

Place the stiffening over the reverse side of the back, fold the turnings over, snipping away where necessary, catch-stitch or herringbone (or stick).

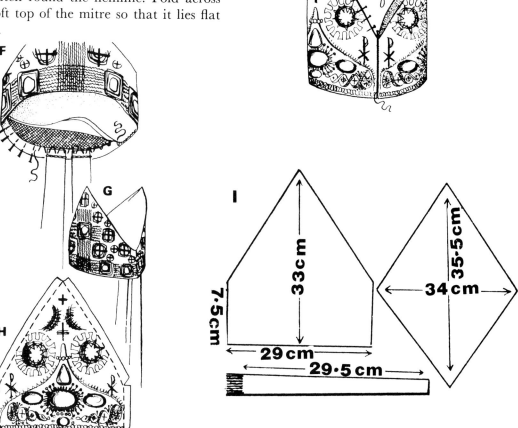

46 Making-up a mitre. Method 2

Make and attach the lappets; cut out the lining, allowing turnings, hem in position. Repeat for the front.

Put the front and back together, right sides out. Overcast the side seams.

Next, fold back the turnings of the gusset (this remains unlined). Match up the points of the gusset with the corresponding points of the mitre, and pin; then pin along each side (*46J*). Overcast and finish with a cord or couching which can also match the side joins.

A slightly stiffened headband, which may be of thin leather, one side threaded with ribbon or narrow braid, can be stitched in round the headline; the ribbon can be drawn up to make it smaller.

This method has the advantage that it can be more easily adjusted to fit the wearer.

THE CASSOCK ALB

The cassock alb (*47*) is an outcome of the discussions held by the Liturgical Commission in 1978 and is the now accepted shape. It is worn with the chasuble or with a stole. The girdle is unnecessary. A belt, about 14 cm wide and fastening with matching buttons can be worn with the cassock-alb as shown. The collar or a cowl replaces the amice.

For the pleats to hang well much depends upon the choice of material, it must have sufficient weight yet it should launder easily. Recommended is the 'Linen Look' polyester viscose obtainable from John Lewis, also the John Lewis polyester 60% and 40% cotton.

The scale for the graph of the pattern for the cassock alb is 1 square to 5 cm and, in this instance, an *allowance* of 1.5 cm *on all seams* of the pattern pieces 1, 2, 3, 4 (*48*) has been *included*.

To save the time spent on neatening the edges, the front and back facings 1 and 2 can be placed upon the material with the selvedge grain running across (the selvedge can then be used for the edge).

47 A white Cassock alb designed by the Rev Leonard Childs. Tailored by Lilian Bedding of the Cathedral Workshop, Derby

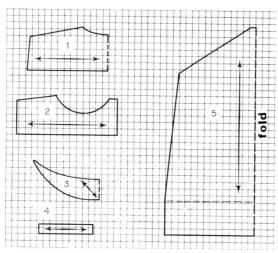

48 Pattern for a cassock alb.
Scale 1 square=5 cm

Place the centre back to a fold; and cut the front double.

The collar, 3: place the centre back of the pattern to a fold on the cross (bias) of the material, cut two.

Facings for the pocket openings, 4, cut four. Here too the selvedge can be used instead of a hem.

The sleeve, 5: turnings of 2.5 cm have been allowed for French seams. And a hem with lay of 15 cm is included.

Place the centre back (*49.6*) (dotted line) to the fold, with the grain of the material. *Turnings* for French seams 2.5 cm *have been included* on both the back and both fronts, also a hem with its lay of 15 cm. The position of the pleats and pocket openings should be marked and should correspond on the back and both fronts. The pattern for the front (*49.7*) is cut double, the straight edge of the front folds can be placed to the selvedge, so avoiding a hem. (This could be cut wider.)

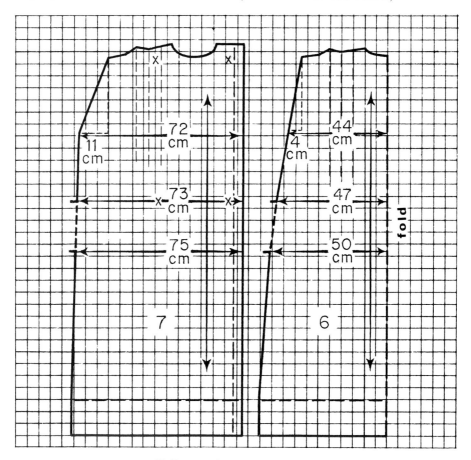

49 Pattern for a cassock alb.
Scale 1 square=5 cm

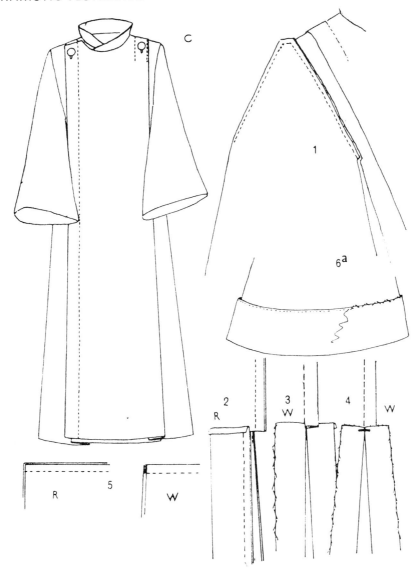

50 Constructing a cassock alb

Mark through the position for the buttons and buttonholes, X on the diagram, and the position for the *Velcro*, the lower X.

Method

With the back and the fronts laid out flatly, fold, pin and tack in the pleats, which should fold outwards towards the sides. Stitch down both edges for about 15 cm at the shoulders.

Pin and tack, then press as each stage is completed.

Join the shoulders with an open seam.

Match the centre top of the sleeve to the shoulder seam, then fit the sleeve top into the armhole (*50.1*) very slightly easing the sleeve. For this a French seam is used, so the wrong sides of the two pieces are put together (*50.5*) (with the right sides outside); make the first row of stitching, trim the edges, fold it over, press, and make the second row of stitching on the wrong side of the garment.

Put each pocket facing with the turning of the cut edge to the side seam line of the garment, and stitch (*50.2*) along on the seam line. Turn over on to the wrong side of the garment, fold back the pocket pieces and catch-stitch (*50.3*). Neaten and then strengthen the ends either by working a little bar (*50.4*) or stitching across.

Next, join the sides, with French seams starting at the sleeve hem and through to the top of the pocket opening, then from the bottom of the pocket opening to the hem.

Stitch down a 5 mm lay around the cut edge of the hem and the sleeves.

Turn up the hems, matching the straight grain and seams. Herringbone or catch-stitch the sleeves and hand-stitch or machine-stitch the bottom hem. (These are wide enough to allow for adjustment to the wearer's height *50.6a*)

Join the shoulder seams of the facing.

To make the collar, put the two collar pieces together, stitch round the outer curve, press, and turn out.

Place the centre back of the collar to the centre back of the garment, pin and tack it to the neckline.

Take the facing, and with right sides together put the centre back over the centre back of the collar and garment. Stitch along the fitting line. Pare down the surplus turning and nick at intervals (*51.6*) then turn the facing over, on to the inside of the garment. Catch the shoulder seams together by hand (*51.7*).

Next, turn over the fold which forms the facing down both sides. (This lies over the yoke facing. It can be cut a little wider than the 5 cm allowed in the pattern.) Turn in the top edges and slip-stitch together, and machine-stitch down, keeping the stitching at the same distance from the edge (*51.7*).

Sew two washable 2.5 cm covered buttons in position on the left front (*51.8*).

Next make two buttonholes 3 mm larger than the button, either by hand or by machine, on the right-hand front (*51.9*).

Sew pieces of *Velcro* to the upper side of the left front and underside of the right front, in the positions marked by the lower

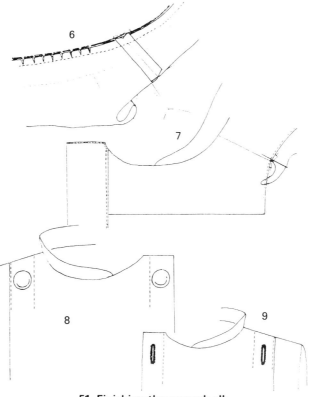

51 Finishing the cassock alb

crosses on the pattern.

Transparent plastic press-studs can be sewn to keep the sleeve-ends together, so that the shirt or other coloured sleeve is not seen.

Roughly three times the total length plus sleeve length will give the amount of material required.

THE ALB

The alb is the long white garment worn under the chasuble; it is caught in at the waist with the girdle.

Design

The diagrams show simple forms.

The alb can have an embroidered border (white or coloured) or a stitched-on apparel around the hem, with embroidered or applied apparels at the cuffs. Alternately, embroidered or fabric apparels can be stitched on to the front and back, a few centimetres up from the hem.

Alternatively there can be rows of drawn thread work at hem and sleeve.

Material

Traditionally white linen, or grease-resistant washable structured fabric such as 90% synthetic fibres and 10% flax. There are opaque fabrics composed of synthetic fibres and viscose, others are 55% synthetic and 45% wool.

A soft material 45% wool and 55% synthetic is of a more open weave and would be suitable for drawn thread work. There are other polyester and cotton mixtures or heavy nylons.

Method 1

For the style shown in *figure 52*, draft out the pattern (*52A*) for the yoke and sleeve. Cut out two front and two back yokes,

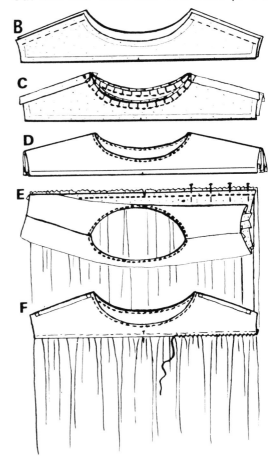

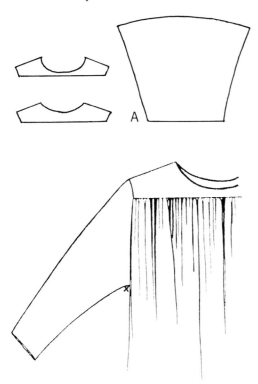

52 Making an alb. Pattern A.
Scale 1 square=5 cm

allowing for turnings. Cut two sleeves, allowing turnings and extra length, according to the arm length of the wearer, plus hem at the cut line. For the front and back take a width of the material for each, according to the width of the fabric. An average length is 140 to 152 cm plus hem, and chest 94 to 114 cm.

Take one front and one back yoke, put the right sides together, stitch along the shoulder seams, press open. Repeat with the other front and back yoke (*52B*).

With the right sides together, take the two yokes, put one over the other, with centre front and centre back corresponding: stitch round the neck, then snip (*52C*). Turn through to the right side and stitch round the neck (*52D*). Turn in and tack the bottom of the inside of the front and back yokes. Run two gathering threads across each width of the material of the alb. Stroke the gathers. Pull it up until it fits the width of the yoke.

Next, with the right side of the front yoke to the right side of the shirring, and matching up the centres, pin, tack and stitch (*52E*). Repeat for the back, then take the lining piece of the yoke, and put it over the stitching, hem it down so that it neatens the setting-in of the gathering. Repeat for the back (*52F*). Sew tapes across the shoulders, for hanging. It may be preferred to leave the lining piece of yoke loose until after setting in the sleeve, then to hem it down all round, and attach the loops. Mark a point 36 cm down from the shoulder seams on the front and back side seams (marked X on the diagram). From this point to the bottom of the alb join the sides with French seams. Snip across the first lay at the top of the seam.

Join the underarm seams of the sleeve, using french seams. Put the centre of the sleeve to the shoulder seam; for a french seam it will be stitched on the right side first, then turned through and stitched on the inside.

Adjust the sleeve and hem lengths, turn up and invisibly hem. If the bottom of the

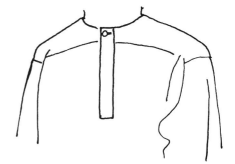

53 An alternative shape which can be adapted from pattern

alb is to be slightly shaped, small darts may be made when turning up the hem.

Figure 53 shows an alternative which can be adapted from this pattern.

Method 2

(***Alb with apparels***) Although this is a traditional alb, it is sometimes still used. It will be noted that the only shaping is on the underarm seam. If there is a centre front seam the neck opening can conveniently be made in the seam. Otherwise the continuous wrap placket is simple to do.

To make the continuous wrap opening of 20 cm, cut a selvedge-way strip twice the length of the opening and twice the finished width, plus turnings. With right sides together, stitch, keeping very close to the edge at the base of the slit (*54.1*). Fold the strip in half, turn in the lay and hem (*54.2*). It may be necessary to stitch a tiny dart at the base of the opening. Press over. *Figure 54.3* shows the finished placket on the right side. Set the main part of the alb into the shoulder bands. Seam up the sides to within 41–46 cm of the shoulder. Gather up each side of the front and the back. Set into the neckband, as for surplice. Next, measure the radius of the button in from the edge, and mark and cut the slit for the buttonhole which measures the diameter of the button, plus 3 mm. If working by hand lay a thread along the edges. Start the buttonhole stitching at the lower left-hand edge, as shown in *figure 54.5*. At the round end overcast 7 or 9 stitches (*54.6*). Then slip the needle into position for stitching the second side; at the square end put three stitches across (54.7), and over this form a bar by making seven or nine buttonhole stitches, or make the buttonhole with the sewing machine. Stitch up the sleeve seam, leaving 10 cm open for the gusset.

Turn in the edges of the gussets to 10 cm square. Fold across diagonally; overcast this into the sleeve and side seams. Adjust the hem and sleeve lengths. Make and lightly stitch on the apparels, as they have to be removed when the alb is laundered.

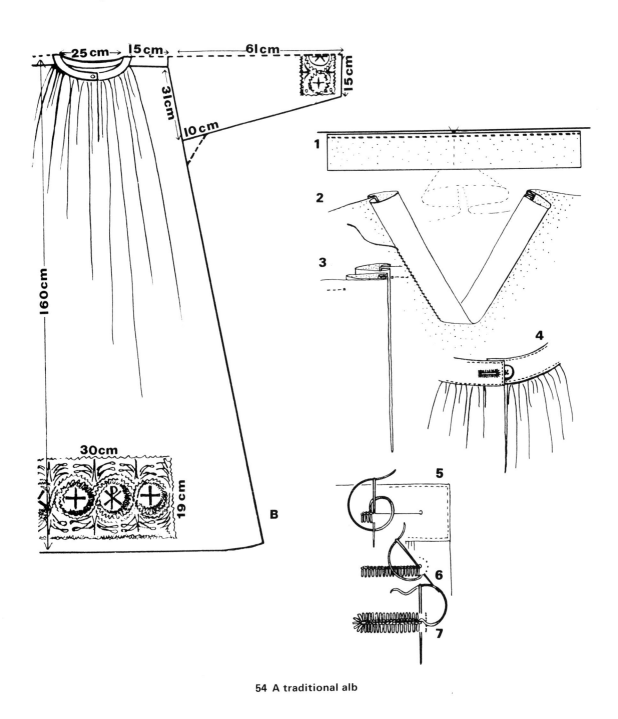

54 A traditional alb

ALTAR LINEN: WHITE WORK EMBROIDERY

FROM earliest times altar linen has been an important requirement of the church, its symbolism, use, and practicability have to be given real consideration. Yet, there is scope and a great need for a fresh approach to designing for this medium because much has changed, in so many ways.

The greatest necessity is that the whole design concept should be on a larger scale, and there is, from the thirteenth and fourteenth centuries in Germany a precedent for this (55). With the nave altar being more generally accepted, the fair linen is seen at close range, therefore there should be more interest in creating decoration which will make an impact. As this type of

stitchery tends to be limited by the thread of the material, the larger scale can be achieved by combining and repeating small individual units, so marking larger areas of texture. Threads of neutral (preferably) colour can enhance the effect.

The wonderfully inventive examples from the past, if studied, should inspire both design and development of hand and machine embroidery.

The characteristic of this stitchery is the limitation imposed by the dependence upon the thread of the linen, yet this makes

55 Altar cloth. White linen embroidered in white. German, early fourteenth century. The Metropolitan Museum of Art. Fletcher Fund 1929 (29.87)

for the pleasure derived from building up the patterns. It is worthwhile to use linen in preference to a substitute, a coarser weave will enable the design to take on a larger scale. Counted thread, pulled and drawn thread work are fascinating to do and can be combined with line stitches, instructions for carrying out a selection are given in the following pages.

Much that was almost sacrosanct in white work has been changed by the introduction and acceptance of the possibilities of machine embroidery. Bolder effects can be produced so much more speedily, and, provided that the methods employed will stand up to machine washing, it will continue to develop.

The embroidered decoration of altar linen starts with the appreciation of the characteristics inherent in stitchery which depends upon the contrast of textures, without colour. From this develops a real feeling for the qualities of solid and open fillings and line stitches.

Before beginning the experimentation it will aid the process if some basic information is acquired, this may be found on the following pages.

Material
Linen is preferable, but there are substitutes to use, provided that the threads can be withdrawn or pulled together.

The choice of suitable embroidery threads is now very limited, it is worth looking for all types when in European countries. Stranded cotton is easily available, linen is difficult to use, but rewarding. For some of the flat, looped, chained, knotted, etc, stitches which are preferably worked in the hand, the texture and roundness of a linen thread is an advantage. DMC No. 20 is fairly coarse, Nos 25 and 35 medium, and No. 40 fairly fine. For working some of the drawn fabric stitches a DMC No. 60 can be used, but for finer pulled and drawn fillings a DMC cotton lace thread No. 200, and for really fine work a reel of machine embroidery thread

No. 30 or 50 is sometimes useful for whipping the foundation.

Satin stitch, trailing, seeding, and for surfaces which need to be smooth with a slight shine, DMC *coton floche à broder* (Red Label) is excellent. No. 25 is fairly coarse, 35 medium and 40 fairly fine. There are, of course, many other sizes of all these threads. The numbers have been selected as a guide. A single thread of CB (Cartier-Bresson) mending is good for fine white embroidery, and Anchor stranded for coloured stitchery upon white. Machine embroidery threads are useful for fine work.

Transferring the design
The more traditional white work cannot be developed free-hand, the old method of pricking and pouncing is still preferable. To do this frame-up or pin out the linen, put the centre of the perforated tracing to the centre of the material, pounce and paint with blue water-colour. Alternatively, if the material is sufficiently transparent, outline the design in ink, put it underneath and in contact with the back of the material; a finer outline can be achieved if a very hard pencil with a sharp point is used instead of a painted line. Where possible longer straight lines which run parallel to the thread of the linen are better tacked instead of traced, also for patterns depending upon the thread of the fabric.

White work line and filling stitches
This type of work has to withstand much hand or machine washing and ironing. This determines the choice and explains the reason for the popularity of satin stitch in the past, and it still has its uses. To execute *satin* stitch (*56A*), straight or diagonal, first making a row of tiny *running* stitches round the outline. If there is to be a padding, this can be of *herringbone* (*56B*) or *chain* (*56C*). To pad, when working in a frame, there are three stages, the first a few laid stitches in the centre, followed by more, crossing the first stitches at right angles, and taken nearly up to the edge in the final layer, the

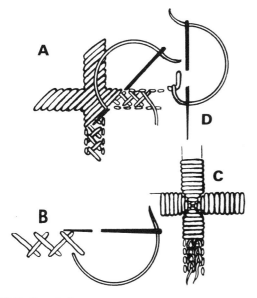

56 Satin stitch

57 Satin stitch contrasted with buttonhole stitch

stitches at right angles, and taken nearly up to the edge in the final layer, the stitches at right angles to the direction of the satin stitches and going right up to the edge. It is important that all the padding should be on the right side and that only a tiny stitch should go through to the back. In making the satin stitches the needle goes right across under the fabric, coming out in position for the next stitch; these should be absolutely even. The spacing of *buttonhole*

stitch can be varied, as can the thread with which it is worked (*56D*).

Satin stitch is sometimes chosen because, when worked in self-colour, it catches the light as the direction of the stitch changes (*58*).

Elementary stitches such as stem (*59A*) can form a solid filling or a wide straight or undulating band when many rows are worked side by side, close together or spaced (*59*). To work stem stitch insert the

58 Detail from a Torah Mantle, illustrating the play of light upon self-coloured satin stitch

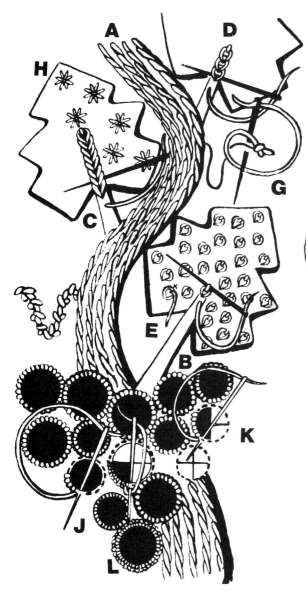

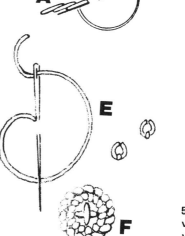

59 Combining various white work stitches

bring it out ahead; each time it passes behind two chain loops (*59C*). *Broad chain* is similar, but instead of going back through the second chain loop, the needle is put through the previous stitch each time (*59D*).

Detached chain stitches are invaluable for producing a regular or irregular powdering upon a surface (*59E*).

Barred buttonhole wheel (*59F*). Instead of working the sixteen stitches always into the same hole as usual, work the first four into one interstice of the fabric, then miss over one thread and work four into the next, and continue in the same way round the circle. Or a double bar may be left in the centre.

In *Broderie Anglaise* it is the pattern, composed of eyelet holes, which is cut away; these should be large enough to show up, yet not too big for laundering. The material used should be closely woven, and the method and stages in the working can be followed from the diagram (*59J*). Outline the shape with small running stitches, pierce with a stiletto for a small eyelet, or (*59K*) cut down and across from the centre for a larger one. Turn back a section at a

needle half way along the previous stitch, keeping the thread consistently above or below the needle.

Heavy chain stitch produces a wider continuous line. Start with a small running stitch, bring the needle out as if for a second, but instead put the needle underneath the running stitch, pull it through and take it down at the point when it last came through. Now bring the needle up a short distance ahead and pass it a second time through the running stitch (*59B*). Again put it down in the same hole and

time, and, using the same working thread, closely overcast or buttonhole stitch (*59L*) through the double material. Fasten off at the back or carry the thread to the next hole. Cut away turnings on the wrong side.

The working of *wheat-ear* stitch can be followed from *figure 60A*. As an outline or repeated as a filling, *coral* stitch is useful; worked from right to left, the needle should be put into the material at right angles to the line and with the thread twisted round, the thumb must be kept over it as the needle is pulled through (*59G*).

To form the stars (*59H*), stitch a cross with another crossing it; catch them down in the centre with a tiny stitch. The first stage in working *chevron* as a line stitch is shown (*60B*), and by adding subsequent rows it forms a filling (*60C*).

Another decorative stitch which is well suited to white work is *Cretan* stitch, as its width can be varied; in the diagram (*60D*) the needle is shown pointing upwards with

the thread to the left; for the next stitch it will be inserted into the upper edge with point downwards; the thread will remain on the left of the needle as it is pulled through. *Whipped run* stitch can be varied according to the thread used (*60E*).

By working *double back* stitch on the wrong side of the material downwards then across (*60F*) over the same number of threads, small raised squares are formed on the right side; arranged side by side they can form a border (*60G*).

Usually *trailing* (*60H*) is worked in a frame. Thread up three threads and make a knot at the end, put the needle in a little beyond the line and bring it out actually on the line; then, using another and finer thread, with tiny satin stitch worked close together, cover the padding threads; at the finish of the line they are taken through to the back where they, and the commencing knot and end are cut off fairly close.

The alternating ridged and open-work

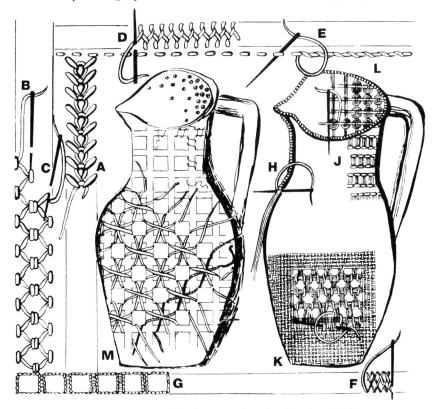

60 A composite diagram showing hand worked stitches with drawn and pulled fillings

stripes showing at the right side (60J) can be obtained by withdrawing slightly fewer threads than those retained. On the wrong side, work double back stitch across the remaining threads; in the second row take up the same groups of threads.

In drawn thread and pulled work the outline must first be completed. The lace filling (60M) can either be used as a pulled, or drawn stitch; if threads are withdrawn each way, for example, 4 and 4, then whip this foundation downwards and across using a fine thread and drawing it up more tightly than is shown in the diagram (61E). (The use of a frame helps to keep the work taut.) Next whip diagonally across (the darkest thread), cross this on the return (the one shaded), repeat in the other direction (60M).

In *figure 60L* the little spirals are worked on the wrong side of facilitate getting from one to another; it can be seen from the diagram that this is done by slipping the needle under the whipping stitches.

If the linen is fairly loosely woven, wave-filling can be worked (this can be followed from *figure 60K*), as a pulled stitch.

To restrict to one stitch the interpretation of a design is an interesting exercise. The size and spacing, also the threads used, can be varied.

Counted thread patterns, when grouped to make larger units are other examples which are characteristic of hand embroidery. The effect obtained with machine embroidery is different, but interesting, if inventive.

Because of the frequent ironing of white

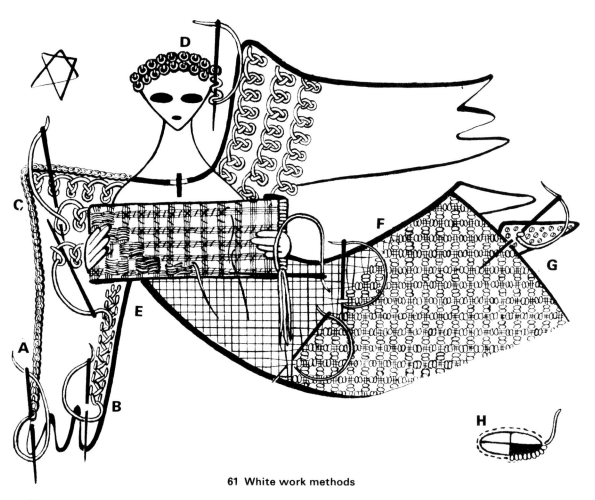

61 White work methods

work it is usual to start stitching by running the thread along the outline; or when a knot is used, this remains on the right side until the thread has been secured by subsequent working; it is then cut off. Fasten on the back by working a few tiny stitches into a nearby outline where they will eventually be covered.

The stitches given in *figure 61*, the Winged Victory, and the other composite diagrams are not exclusive to white work, but they are very suitable.

The *chain* stitch both in its simple form and in its variations is a useful outline stitch (*61A*).

The *single (or double) feather* stitch is effective when sewing cotton is used; it is executed by placing the thread under the needle from left to right, then for the next stitch on the left of the line the thread will go under the needle from right to left; the position shown in *figure 61B*, the left-hand thumb will be kept over the thread whilst the needle is pulled through. It should be stitched towards the worker.

Rosette chain is invaluable for giving a broken or decorative edge; a linen thread produces the best results. Having brought the thread up at the right-hand end of the line, pass it across to the left and hold it with the thumb. Put the needle into the fabric and bring it up through the loop formed by the thread and pull it through (*61C*). Then pass the needle under the thread to the right, as shown below. Repeat at regular intervals. *French knots*, massed or

singly are effective. To commence, bring the thread through, hold it taut with the left hand and encircle the needle twice (*61D*). Whilst holding the thread, revolve the needle and put it down close to where it came up, and keeping the thumb over the twists, pass the needle through to the back. When not worked in a frame the material has to be held between the second and third finger of the left hand.

In *figure 61E* the beginning of a woven pattern upon a whipped foundation, is shown. (It will be seen that this is the reverse side, as it is easier to work on.) This can be combined with other stitches; also the direction of the weaving can be varied. A lace thread is generally used for these drawn thread fillings.

Double faggot stitch is worked by completing first one then another stitch over two horizontal threads (*61F*) (shown above), and passing the needle diagonally behind the intersection of the two warp and weft threads making first one then another stitch over two vertical threads (shown below), covering the ground with diagonally stitched rows. A fairly fine thread should be used otherwise the perforations will not show. *Seeding* produces graduated massing and irregularity by the spacing and size of the stitches. To work, make a tiny back stitch, then another on top of first (*61G*) to make a little raised spot. And at (*61H*) is shown Broderie Anglaise.

For the drawn thread filling (*62A*) work small running stitches around the outline.

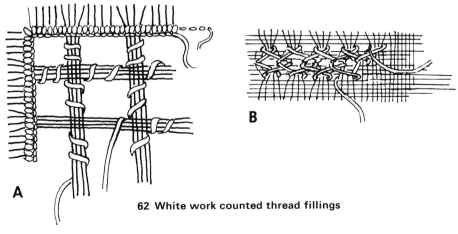

62 White work counted thread fillings

Then work buttonhole stitches. Withdraw four threads leaving in four in both directions. Whip downwards and across using a very fine thread as shown. This can form the foundation for many stitches.

Figure 62B This pulled filling is worked on the wrong side, using double back stitch. This forms raised ridges on the right side.

Figure 63A The edges of cut work are stitched with little running stitches, the material is cut into the corners and folded back as in the diagram, then whipped, the turnings are then cut away on the back.

Figure 63B This filling is composed of small squares of shadow work. Withdraw two threads in both directions, leaving in ten threads, work double back stitches down then across on the wrong side.

Figure 63C First lay a number of threads lengthwise. Across these are worked stitches at regular intervals. Start-ing at the base, lines of stem stitches are worked only over the transverse stitches; called *raised stem band*.

Figure 64A One thread of the fabric is withdrawn and ten threads left in both directions, as will be seen in the diagram, each stitch is taken into the same hole in the centre and pulled fairly tightly, two of the fabric threads are left between each stitch.

The edges for cut work are either overcast as at (*63A*), or finished with a buttonhole edge. The fillings are all based upon buttonholed bars composed of threads of the fabric (*64B*) or can be made from long stitches taken from one side to the other. These bars can either be woven (*64C*) or overcast as at (*64D*). It will be seen that lace like patterns can be built up from these beginnings as shown at (*65C*). The techniques referred to can also be seen in (*65A,B,C and D*).

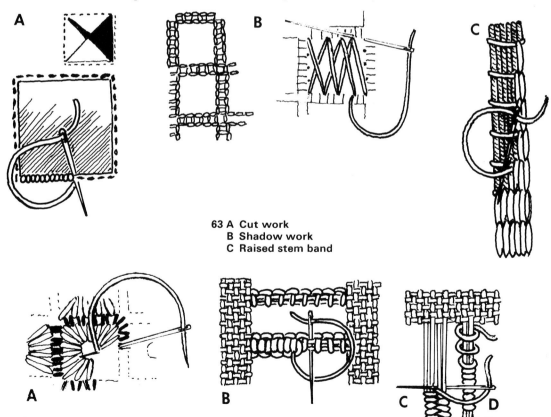

63 A Cut work
   B Shadow work
   C Raised stem band

64 A Drawn thread work
   B Button holed bars
   C Woven bars for cut work
   D Overcast bars for cut work

THE FAIR LINEN CLOTH
(*figure 65*)

This example illustrates many of the points being considered, it is intended for use on a wider, free-standing stone altar, without a frontal. Therefore it was designed to be bold and large in scale and texture, in order to make an impact. To achieve the desired contrast of tone, the linen was hand woven so that drawn thread and pulled work could be juxtaposed with the areas of applied opaque white linen, and this would throw into relief the cut work and Broderie Anglaise. The surface stitches give additional texture.

Details are shown overleaf. The small squares of drawn thread are worked by

65(a) One end of a Fair Linen (91 cm deep) designed and worked by Beryl Dean. This illustrates the repetition of small single units to make large-scale areas and shows a selection of coarser, mainly linen threads on hand woven linen

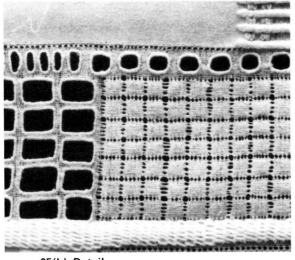

65(b) Detail

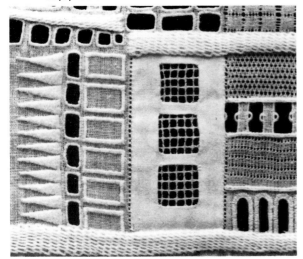

65(c) Detail

65(d) Detail

withdrawing four threads and leaving four in both directions, then whipping with a fine thread. This can be used as the basis for many patterns. The squares are let into the opaque linen.

At *65A* is shown one of the pulled stitches, it is usually worked on the reverse side in rows. But here it is on the right side, a very fine thread is used, and it is over more then three threads of material. Both overcast and buttonhole edges to the cut away shapes are used. To achieve the very sharp points of the satin stitch it is essential to make tiny running stitches or fine split stitch around the edges, before working the satin stitches.

The square holes shown in the detail (*65B*) are worked in the usual way by first doing little running stitches round the edge, then cutting into the corners of the square and turning the edge back with the needle, the edge is overcast as in *figure 63A* and the surplus turning cut away on the reverse side.

A thick cotton thread (from Sweden) was used for the heavy raised stem stitch band (*65B, 63C*). The filling composed of small squares (*63B*) is worked on the reverse side, first withdraw two threads in each direction, then make double back stitches down and across, taking up two threads of the linen.

The filling *64A* and 65(b) shows a variation of eye stitch.

Counted Thread Filling Stitches. For the 'burden' stitch, first cover the ground with equally spaced laid threads, to the thread of the material where possible, make two satin stitches side by side over the first and second foundation rows (*68A*), then work another two over the second and third rows, repeat over the first and second, and so on. When single stitches are worked over two threads of the fabric without the laid stitches, it is called *Morris darning* or *brick stitch.*

One of an immense variety of satin stitch open fillings is shown in *figure 68B.*

For the filling shown in *figure 68C* groups

66 Chasuble for the Lenten array. The Sarum Group, designed by Jane Lemon for Salisbury Cathedral

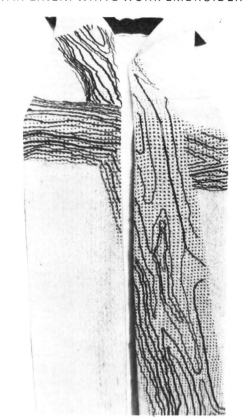

67(a) Stole for the Lenten array. The Sarum Group, designed by Jane Lemon for Salisbury Cathedral

67(b) Detail

of satin stitches are threaded with a coarser round thread. For these and other filling stitches, simple shapes are preferable, as they allow the pattern to show to advantage.

Four-sided stitch (*68D*) is frequently used as an all-over background coverer, throwing the pattern into relief.

Single Faggot stitch (*68E*) is also an all-over filling, it is worked obliquely and the square is executed in two rows. The needle is shown working the first line, and the

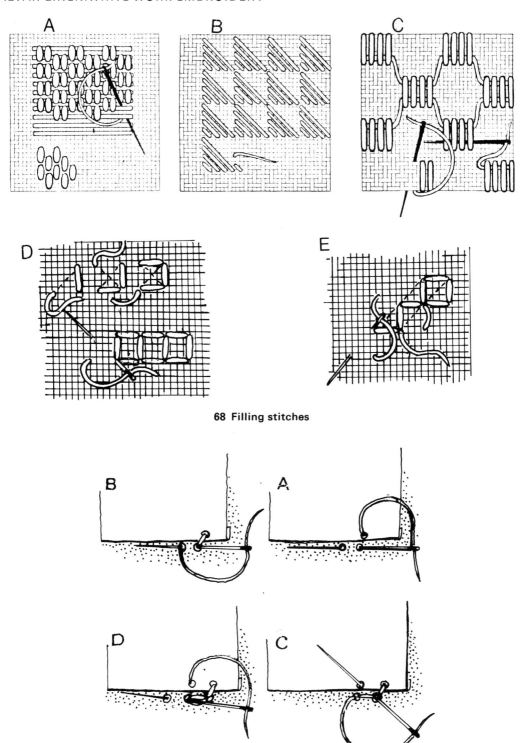

68 Filling stitches

69 Pin stitching

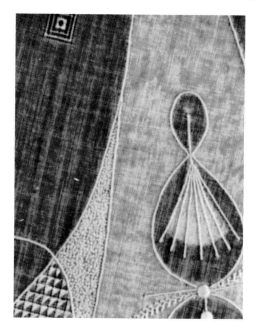

70 A–D Details from a larger piece of white work. Stitches and fillings described in the text

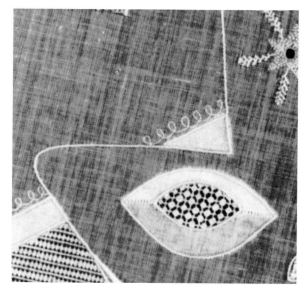

loosened stitch and end of thread constitute the second line, the dotted line indicates the back of the stitch. The thread must be drawn tightly, and the most satisfactory result is obtained on a loosely woven fabric.

This excellent Lenten set designed by Jane Lemon (*66* and *67*) shows how one stitch, together with couched threads, can be used with imagination. Double faggot makes an effective background when the pattern remains in the fabric.

Details from a larger piece of white work (*70*); because the background is semi-transparent, it was possible to introduce various degrees of density by putting one or more layers underneath and working outlines, mainly trailing around the shapes, whereas the opaque linen used in the fair linen (*65*) was applied on the surface with pin stitching (*69*) and handkerchief hem stitch, for which two threads are withdrawn when on

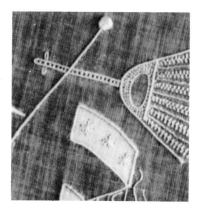

a straight edge, and the hem-stitching (*71* and *73*) is only worked on one side, picking up two threads at each stitch. The areas must be kept small, otherwise it will not wash well.

Many of the fillings, etc, can be adapted for machine embroidery.

The preparation and treatment of hems

When making up altar linen the finishing of the hems calls for special attention. The most straightforward method is, or course, the ordinary hem, but as a ridge shows after laundering, it is not entirely satisfactory.

Hem-stitching (*73*) is the conventional finish, and, as it is still widely used the following directions for its preparation may be of assistance:

1 For a 2.5 cm hem finish, allow 3 cm all round the article.
2 Spread the material out, measure 6 cm inwards from each edge and mark with a pin.
3 Slightly lift and pull one thread in each direction so that they meet at the corner (*71A*).
4 Repeat at the diagonally opposite corner. The point at which these threads meet those of the first corner forms the position of the third and fourth corners.
5 Snip at each intersection and withdraw these threads, then draw out as many more as are required.
6 Fold 6 mm underlay and turn up the hem to the edge of the withdrawn threads. For a rectangle, arrange the opposite long sides first, then the shorter.

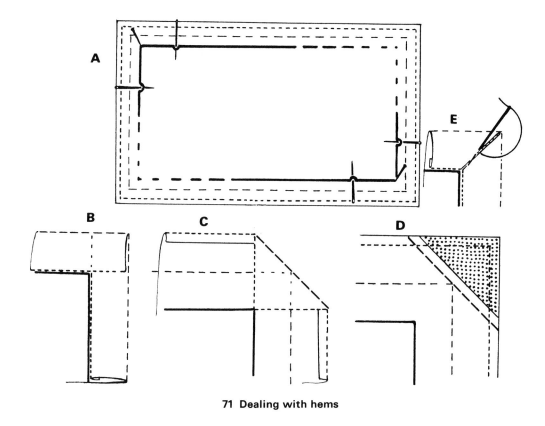

71 Dealing with hems

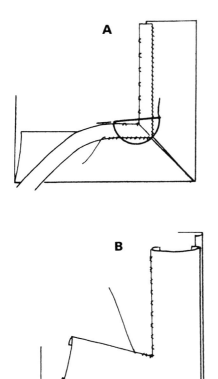

72 Stitching a facing

7 Slightly flatten the hems arranged as in *figure 71B*.

8 Then re-fold the corner (*71C*), making a crease.

9 Measure out 6 mm from this crease and cut off the shaded portion (*71D*). Turn in this 6 mm at the dotted line.

10 Re-fold the corner into a mitre, and slip stitch on the wrong side (*71E*).

Many designs are planned to have a perfectly plain treatment for the edge. Where a certain emphasis would be an advantage a feature may be made of a length of hem-stitching just where it is needed; this may, for instance, be terminated with a small raised circle of an eyelet hole. This raises its own problem because, if the remainder of the hem is simply hemmed down the resultant ridge would spoil the effect. One way to overcome this is

by omitting the underlay. Fold the hem into position, cut and stitch the mitred corner. Then pin and tack into place on the edge of the hem a narrow linen tape (folded diagonally at the corners). Attach it with hemming and lightly catch or slip hem the edge of the tape to the linen (*72A*), using fine sewing cotton as it is stronger.

Sometimes it is preferable to face up the edges on the reverse side with a fine, thin material cut to shape (*72B*).

For a narrow fringed hem, withdraw a couple of threads at the required measurement from the edge all round. Hem-stitch on the inner side only, then withdraw the remaining threads to form a fringe. A few strands can either be woven or knotted in at the corners.

Hem-stitching is the most usual method of finishing hems. When this is worked on one side only – two threads are taken out and two picked up each time – it is known as *handkerchief hem-stitching* and it is much used for church linen (although one needs to avoid automatically finishing all hems in this way, as it draws attention from the main interest to the outer edges). With the hem held towards the worker and the wrong side uppermost, put a knot in the thread and start with a long stitch lying along the top of the hem, and, bringing the needle up at the left-hand corner (*73A*), it will then pass diagonally across as the needle is put from right to left behind the first group of two threads. The needle is then brought out and inserted vertically as at (*73B*), ready to continue. Joining in a new thread is shown at (*73C*); when the hem stitches have secured the old and new threads they, like the commencing knot, are cut off on the right side. For spoke stitch four threads are usually withdrawn and the same groups of four are picked up and hem-stitched on both side. (*73D*) shows this from the right side of the work. For split group stitch, four threads are picked up on the first side, and on the second two threads from each group, so that a chevron is formed; its appearance on the right side is illustrated at (*73E*). Italian stitch or double hem stitch is similar. Draw out one thread, leave in three and draw out another one, working on the back make a back stitch over three threads at the bottom left-hand space (*73F*), and then take up the same three in the top space (*73G*), pass the needle vertically behind three threads (*73H*).

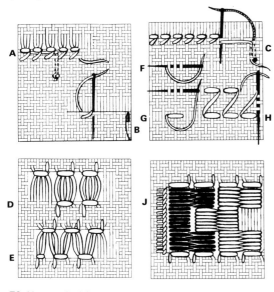

73 Hem-stitching

A woven hem is both ornamental and strong. To work first pull the top and bottom threads of the border, then strengthen the ends with buttonhole stitching over small running stitches. Next, cut the horizontal threads close to the heading of the buttonhole stitching at both ends, and withdraw. (An alternative method is to make a cut vertically down the centre of the border and withdraw the horizontal threads to the left and right to the points marked for the two ends, then threading up each thread in turn, darn it back for a few stitches into the material and cut off on the back.) The groups of threads can be hem-stitched or the weaving can be worked over groups of threads picked up by the needle.

Figure 73J gives a simple woven border which, when repeated, would entirely cover the vertical threads. There is scope for the invention of many designs of greater complexity. This type of work looks very rich when other embroidered patterns are introduced as a part of the scheme.

Another suitable hem for church linen is made by turning the hem over on to the right side, and working tiny overcast stitches over a thread, such as crochet cotton, which gives a raised, corded effect.

The finishing and cleaning of linen embroidery

Before taking the work out of the frame, cover the back with a damp cloth and press with a hot iron.

Using several layers of thick blanket covered with a clean cloth, embroidery which has not puckered can be placed face down and pressed on the back using a damp cloth, before making-up.

Work which is clean but puckered can be pinned out, with the grain of the material straight down and across. First cover a drawing board (or something suitable) with two or three layers of blanket and a clean white cloth. Place the work face downwards and stretch it out; pinning the edges with drawing-pins, dampen, and leave to dry for twenty-four hours.

When the embroidery has become grubby during the working, before making it up, prepare a basin of hot suds or mild detergent and dip it up and down, but do not rub or squeeze. Rinse quickly and put the work face down on a well-padded surface which has over it two layers of clean dry cloth. Cover the reverse side of the work with another cloth and dry it off with a hot iron.

Altar linen is usually ironed-up wet on the wrong side over several layers of thick blanket and a clean cloth.

When there is embroidery, hand is preferable to machine washing.

74 Planning the decoration of the Fair Linen Altar cloth ▶

The Fair Linen
or
Altar Cloth

The Christian altar is the table around which people gather to celebrate the Eucharist. The Canon Law of the Church of England states: ' . . . it shall be covered in the time of Divine Service with a covering of silk or other decent stuff, and with a fair linen cloth at the time of celebration . . . '. In the Bible it is linen which is specifically mentioned. The Fair Linen cloth is an interesting piece of embroidery to plan as the ends can have handsome borders, and deep knotted fringes formed by the threads of the material. The stitchery can include

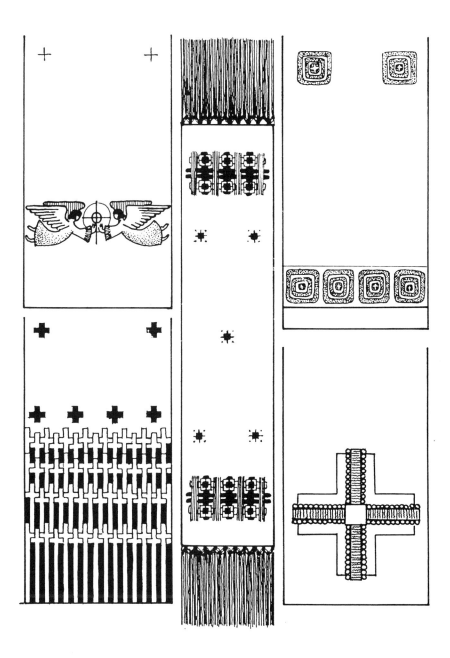

pulled and drawn thread work. Alternatively there can be a wide hem and larger motif in the centre of both ends. See examples in *figure 74*.

Five small crosses are also obligatory – one in the centre and at each corner of the mensa, when in position on the altar. In the Roman Catholic Church, these crosses are not used, but a narrow flat border can be worked along both long sides.

The free-standing nave altar is sometimes wider, and is often of stone and without an altar frontal, therefore there is much scope for wide, decorative ends to the cloth (*65*). There is every reason to use a coarser linen, as this facilitates a freer approach to a larger scale of working either by hand or machine embroidery.

75 Two sets comprising pall, corporal and lavabo towel from Cologne, and a pall from Spain

Measurements

The fair linen measures the exact width of the altar when finished, and it should hang almost to the ground at each end; when cutting, the width of the hems plus narrow lays must be added.

Therefore, that for a small altar (183 cm × 99 cm high × 61 cm wide) might measure (finished) 183 cm + 95 cm + 95 cm + hems × 61 cm + hems.

Method

If the embroidery is to be worked in a frame, the remaining length has to be rolled round the roller of the frame; alternately a clamp-on tambour frame may be more convenient.

Next, neaten the long hems, then the short. There are several decorative methods, which, with careful thought, can be used more imaginatively than by doing the same treatment all round. For example, a

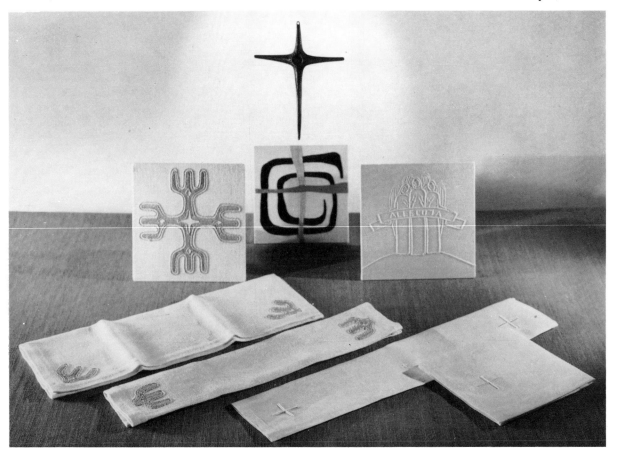

very narrow needle-woven border might be taken down the long sides with a wider panel at each end, developed by the addition of other stitchery.

If a plainer edge, with a wide hem at the ends is preferred, then one of the methods given in *figure 73* can be adapted to the requirements.

The decoration of the *credence cloth* should match the altar cloth. The width is that of the credence table and the ends hang down generously at each end.

THE PALL

When dressing the chalice, the folded purificator is first placed across the chalice; over this the paten (in the diagram this just shows on one side), with the priest's wafer upon it; this is covered by the pall, which is a stiffened square (*76*). Sometimes a second corporal is used instead; it is

folded in three both ways and forms a pall; it has a cross embroidered in the centre, and is folded with this uppermost.

The pall is used in the Roman Catholic Church, but not always in the Church of England.

Design
The pall is planned as a part of the set of altar linen. Generally derived from a cross (which may be quite small), a sacred monogram or Passion symbol; which ever it is, it is placed centrally. Preferably the design should be readable whichever way it faces. It is usually embroidered in white, but sometimes red or blue. It is sometimes advisable to avoid trailing stitch, as it is almost impossible to get the usual size of electric iron inside the pall to press the back of the embroidery.

76 The Pall

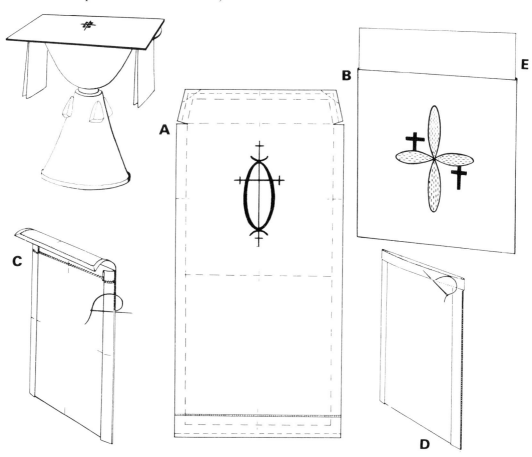

Measurements

Usually 15 cm, but can be from 10 to 16.5 cm square, depending on the size of the paten.

Material

Fine white linen; also a square of cardboard, perspex or plastic, for stiffening, which may or may not be covered. Alternatively folds of stiffened (with starch) linen can be used.

Method 1

This is on the principle of an envelope.

1 Tack out the shape, complete and press the embroidery.
2 Cut, allowing turnings and lay at one end, and shape the other end slightly inwards, allowing a narrow turning and little lay to form the flap. Snip as shown in the *figure 76A*.
3 Remove threads, turn down hems, work hem stitching (*73*).
4 Cut across the corners of the flap, fold down turnings, arrange mitres, tack hem and press.
5 Fold back side turnings, and with right sides together, fold at the base, overcast the sides together (*76C*).

Turn out and insert stiffening; tuck in the flap.

Method 2

Prepare as for *method 1*, but without the flap, allowing for hem and lay at both ends. Withdraw threads, if there is to be hem stitching.

1 Overcast the sides together on reverse side.
2 Turn down hem around the opening and hem (*76D*), or hem-stitch. Turn out.

Figure 76E shows the right side of a pall with the stiffening (which is always slightly smaller) protruding.

Method 3

This is composed of a single embroidered square with edges neatened in some suitable way; with little buttonholed bars worked across each corner, at the back.

Slip the covered stiffened square under the bars.

Method 4

1 Take two squares of linen (one embroidered), but, allowing turnings all round each.
2 Fold the turnings back on both sides. Place reverse sides together.
3 Put the stiffening between the two squares and overcast round the four edges.

One side has to be unpicked and restitched after washing.

THE CORPORAL

The chalice stands upon the corporal in the middle of the altar. When not in use it is folded in three both ways and kept in the burse or corporal case. In the Church of England two corporals are occasionally used instead of one, and a pall or a chalice veil. It is the most sacred item of church linen, as the Consecration of the Elements takes place on the corporal.

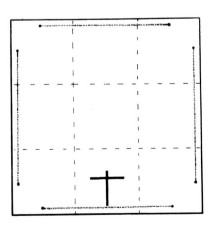

77 The Corporal

Design

The design is planned as part of the set.

One simple or more elaborate cross placed in the centre of one side; this should not exceed one ninth of the total size (77). Sometimes four smaller crosses in the corners. Raised satin stitch, because it causes an uneven surface, and drawn thread work are unsuitable stitches; the latter because particles of the Host might adhere.

Measurements

A square of from 46 to 60 cm, but usually 48 or 50 cm in the Church of England and about 53 cm in the Church of Rome.

Material

White linen; this need not be fine.

When there are two corporals both are of the same linen; the second one has the cross in the centre, with or without corner crosses or borders, but none should take up more than one ninth of the whole.

When another corporal made of fine cambric or linen lawn takes the place of the chalice veil, and is used as a covering after the Consecration, it is from 50 to 60 cm square, and can be embroidered all over or as a border with a central ornament; colour may be used for the embroidery. Although lace is often used on altar linen, it is most unsuitable and seems quite wrong in this context.

Method

Complete the embroidery. Allowing for the width of the hem plus a narrow lay, cut a square to the thread of the linen.

If it is to be invisibly hemmed down with mitred corners, follow the method given for fair linen cloths.

Should the inevitable hem-stitched hem (73) be decided upon, perhaps some original arrangement can be introduced.

Provided that it will launder well, is flat, and will wear, some other possible hem treatment can be tried out. Suggestions are given in the section on Linen Embroidery.

THE PURIFICATOR

The purificator is used for drying the Holy Vessels during the Celebration (75). Purificators are folded in three lengthwise.

Design

One small embroidered cross in the centre or at one corner.

Measurements

About 23 cm × 30 cm, or 30 cm × 36 cm. In the Roman Catholic Church 23 cm × 46 cm, or 30 cm × 46 cm, or 33 × 50 cm is more usual.

Material

Linen, or Birds' eye diaper. Stitched in white, though sometimes in colour.

Method

Cut, allowing for the edge treatment.

1 A narrow hem all round. This is the most usual finish.
2 Hemmed down sides (narrow), hem-stitched hems across the top and bottom (wide).
3 Or the sides can have the wider hems.
4 A fringe about 2.5 cm wide across the narrow ends. For this withdraw about three threads of the fabric, and hem-stitch on one side, then withdraw the remainder of the threads to form the fringe. Repeat for the other end.

Make a narrow hem along the long sides.

THE LAVABO TOWEL

Used for drying the priest's fingers, after he has washed them before the Consecration.

Design

There many be a little decoration above the hems, with or without a small cross at the ends in the centre.

Measurements

60 cm × 26 to 38 cm. Made of linen or substitute.

In the Roman Catholic Church, about 23 cm × 46 cm, or 38 cm, or 41 cm × 50 cm, and made of linen diaper. Fold in three lengthwise.

Method

Narrow hem down long sides, with wide hem, hem-stitched or a hem-stitched fringe.

THE COMMUNION CLOTH

Used in the Roman Catholic Church, and intended for catching falling fragments of the Sacred Host, therefore the embroidery is very restrained.

It is also called the *Houseling Cloth*, but is now seldom used. The length depends upon the length of the altar rails, and the decoration matches that of the fair linen cloth.

THE ALTAR DUST COVER

This is made of coarse coloured linen.
One arrangement is to have one narrower runner under the crucifix and candles, and a wider one to cover the remaining width of the altar; both are cut a little larger than the fair linen cloth.

Narrow hems all round each.

The credence table has a similar dust cover.

THE SURPLICE I

Design

For this surplice (*78*) the sleeves can be square, as shown in the lay-out, or pointed, and instead of having the fullness reduced by gathering (*79*), it can be smocked.

Material

Traditionally white linen, it can be cotton, 137 cm wide, or one of the many man-made mixtures which are washable.

Measurements

From the lay-out (*78.2*), it will be seen that the two sleeves come out side-by-side from 137 cm material. Decide the length of the surplice, plus allowance for hems, add to this the 1.8 m for the sleeves; the total required will be about 5 m, as additional length gives a better proportion.

Method

Cut off the 1.8 m for the sleeves, cut it down the centre (selvedge way); the sleeves are then folded across at the dotted line,

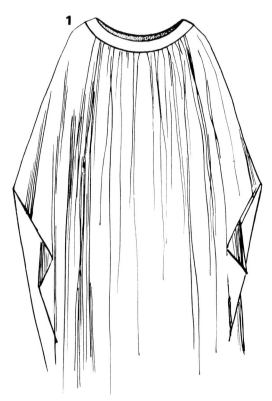

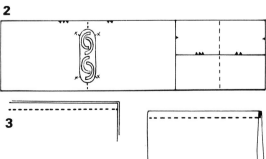

78 Surplice I

the bottom edges (one notch) are seamed together. French seams can be used, *figure 78.3* . Put the wrong sides together, stitch (on the right side) the width of the seam away from the edge, press open, turn on to the wrong side, stitch the width of the seam from the edge. Take the longer piece of material, from the centre mark out an oval for the neck about 25 cm wide and starting and ending about 10 cm from the selvedges (these form the shoulders). Cut the four semicircles for the neck band out of this piece of material (they just come out with turnings).

Join two semicircles together at the shoulders, repeat for the other two. Put the right sides together, stitch round the neck line, snip, press open (*79.4*). Turn through to the right side, stitch on the edge (this gives added strength). Across the neck the opening should measure about 25 cm. Fold in the turnings on the outside of both circles, tack. Mark the position for the gathers (X) on the diagram. Run in two or three gathering threads, keeping the stitches under each other, pull up the gathers, and stroke them; for this use the point of the needle, pressing each gather to form a little pleat. When finished spread out the fullness, and put the centre to the centre of the yoke (*79.5*). Stitch at the right side of the yoke only, holding back the inside. The back is done in the same way.

Turn on to the wrong side, and hem down the yoke (*79.6*). This will have reduced the 140 cm width to 68.5 cm, approximately. Now take one sleeve, put the centre fold to the fold for the shoulder, match-up the corresponding marks and stitch the seam. Repeat for the other sleeve.

Complete the remainder of the side skirt seams, turn up the bottom hem, slightly shaping it at the sides, and hem the sleeves.

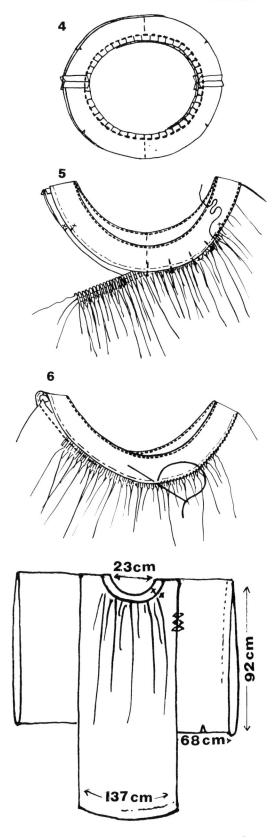

79 Surplice I

THE SURPLICE II

Design

The shape of this surplice is of a later origin. The sleeves are full and pointed (*80A*).

Material

Washable substitutes for linen such as heavy nylon.

Draft out the pattern and mark in the numbered points. (If these figures are also attached after the pieces have been cut out, it will facilitate the putting together.)

Cut one front and one back pattern piece, and two gussets and side panels, also two neck pieces (four if there is a join).

Method

Put number 1 of the gusset to 1 at the bottom of the cut in the side panel.

Match up 2 of the gusset to 2 at the bottom of the cut in the side panel. Stitch *80B*.

Put number 4 at the point of the side panel to 4 on the front.

Join the side-front seam from 4 to 11.

Fix together 6 at the neck of the front, and 6 at the neck of the sleeve, then 4 and 4 on the sleeve seam, 2 and 2 to 7 and 7 (*80C*).

To fix in the back of the sleeve.

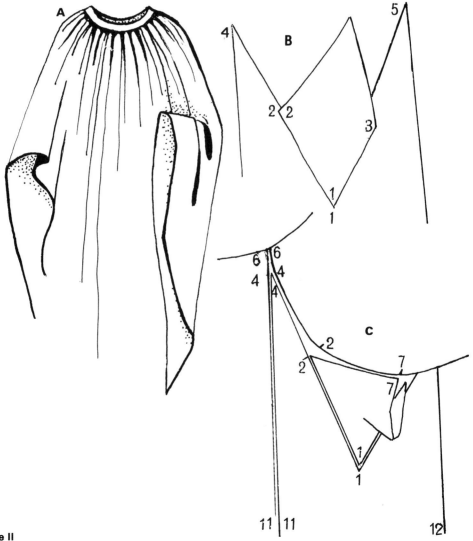

Match up 3 and 3, and 5 on the back sleeve seam to 5 at the point of the back panel.

Stitch from 7 through 3 to 5.

Put the back side-seam of the garment 8 at the neck line, to 8 on the back seam of the sleeve, through 5 and 5, to 12 and 12. Stitch.

Repeat for the second sleeve, remembering to reverse.

A gathering thread is stitched round the neck from centre front and centre back.

The neck is finished as at (79.5,6).

Hem bottom of surplice and make a narrow hem around the sleeve forming a point at 10.

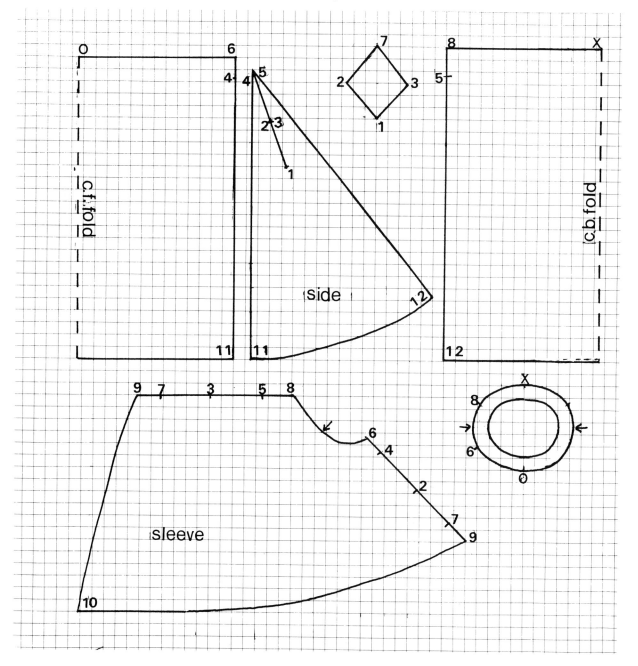

81 Surplice II. Scale 1 square=5 cm

The Cotta

The very short cotta is generally considered to be degenerate, but one very simple example is shown by the heavy lines in *figure 84*. The dotted lines show the variation.

But the same principle can be applied by adapting the pattern for a surplice the average length is 1 metre, it can be longer, and the sleeves are longer (*84* and *85*) small dotted lines.

Cut double, having first estimated the amount required for two or three pleats or gathers. The width of the hems has to be added.

If there is to be decorative hem-stitching,

82 Surplice (cotta). Drawn threadwork stitched in grey

a fabric of synthetic fibres and viscose, or other fabric imitating linen is suitable, as the necessary threads can be withdrawn.

For the yoke, the right sides of the fabric are put together. Stitch round the neck, nick into the corners, turn out, stitch again on the right side. Fold narrow turnings around the yoke pieces and tack. Arrange pleats or pull up gathers.

Join the sleeves and side seams, join sleeves to seams.

Taking the right side of one yoke, match up the centres, set the two or three pleats or gathers into the yoke, also the top of the sleeve, repeat for the other side, and the back.

Neaten by putting the lining yoke over, and hem in place. The process is the same as shown in *figure 79.6*.

Turn up the hems and work the hem-stitching (*73*). If absolutely accurately measured it can be done at the beginning.

If invisibly hemmed, the hemline may be shaped.

If preferred the top of the sleeve and armhole may be shaped.

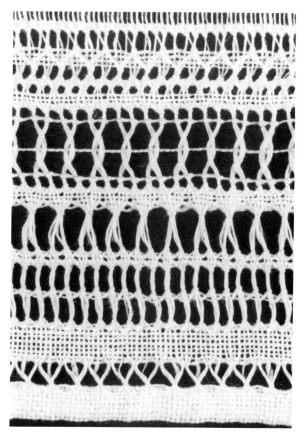

83 Drawn threadwork hems and borders

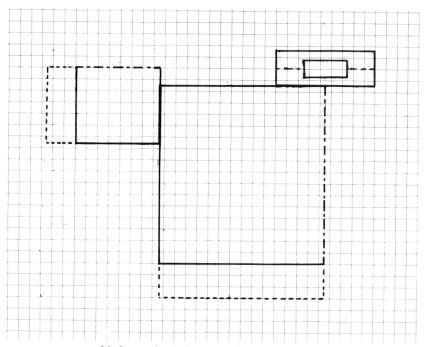

84 Cotta. Scale 1 square=5 cm. Adaptation from surplice

85 Surplice

CHOIR BOY'S RUFF

For an average neck size cut 2 strips 35.5 cm plus turnings × 5.5 cm plus turnings. Neck band, selvedge runs along the length (*86B*).

Cut 1 strip for the ruff, selvedge downwards, 75 cm + hems × 6 cm plus turnings (*A*).

Cut 1 piece for the shaped yoke plus 1.5 cm hems plus 5 mm turning at neck line (*C*).

Method

A pure cotton will launder and the pleats will keep in place.

Stitch an 8 mm hem around the outside of the yoke, arranging sharp points (*87A*).

Snip at intervals at the neck line.

Starting from the centres, put the outside of the yoke to the underside of one neck band, and stitch (*87B*).

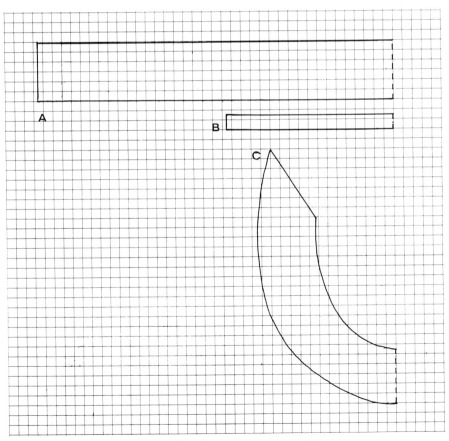

86 Choir boy's ruff. 1 square = 5 cm. Add turnings and hems when cutting (average size)

Stitch a 3 mm hem along the ruff (*87C*).

Mark out the pleats 11 mm apart and 6 mm deep. Fold the pleats and stitch (*87D*) at the neckline. The exact length can be adjusted when the turnings at the ends are made.

Set the wrong side of the pleated ruff (note the hems, in the diagram) into right side of the neck band (*87E*) and stitch.

Fold in the turnings of the second neck band strip.

Place it over the back of the neck band, stitch (*87F*). (Note that the neck band protrudes a little at the end of one side, this forms a neater fastening.)

Turn in the ends and stitch.

Traditionally the ruff was fastened with a washable button and hand-worked buttonhole, now it would be a machine-stitched one, but it is more likely that it would be fastened with small pieces of *Velcro*.

87 Choir boy's ruff

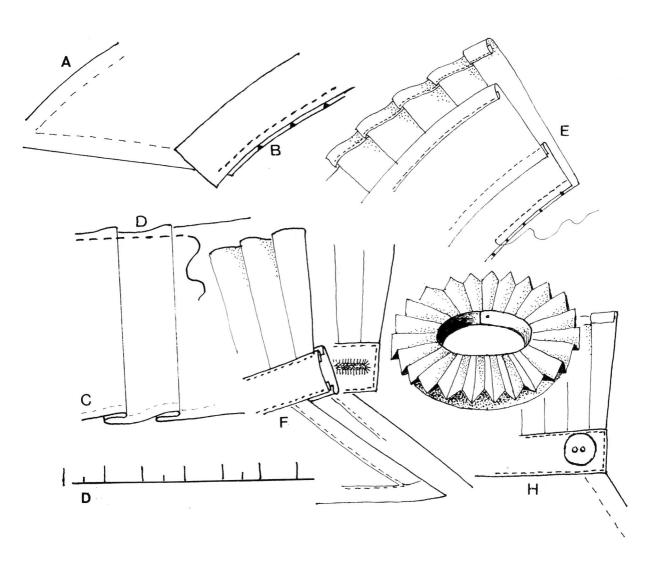

CHURCH FURNISHINGS

BANNERS AND HANGINGS

THERE is tremendous scope for a vigorous and original approach to designing a banner or hanging, the subject can be treated with originality and the colour scheme may be of particular interest because the impact must be instantaneous.

A well-proportioned shape with good clear lines is preferable to the familiar befringed and tasselled banners with the collection on points, curves and angles with which they are embellished.

When positioned in the church, a banner is usually viewed from some distance; it is above eye level then and when used for processions, it may only be glimpsed for a few moments. There are occasions when several banners are seen together. These limitations determine the character when the design is being planned, as it is essential to decide what is to be important, and to emphasise this by making it large and bold, and to eliminate unnecessary or meaningless detail.

If lettering is to appear on the front it should be planned as an integral part of the design, and must be good and well spaced. It is often preferable to put the wording on the reverse side as this is also seen and there is sufficient space for it to be legible.

Material
A fairly heavy material will hang well (although the interlining makes possible the use of lighter ones). A fine or a rough surfaced woollen or a mixture, in dress or furnishing fabric, has interesting possibilities as a background for applying smooth-surfaced materials. For the conventional approach there are Masonic silks or grosgrain, etc. Damasks and brocades seem particularly unsuitable as the light catches and emphasises the woven pattern.

Used in the right way a fringe can make a good finish to the base of a banner.

Poult, taffeta, corded silk, polonaise or glazed cotton, or any other firm fabric, is suitable for lining.

Measurements
Proportion is most important. The length can be more than twice the width (a convenient size is 114 cm or more by 76 cm, there is now a tendency towards longer, narrower, banners. The figure or other subject should be placed with a good space below it

88 'Spire' hanging (length about 3 m). The Sarum Group, designed by Jane Lemon, for Salisbury Cathedral

89 Hanging (6 m × 2.7 m) by Judy Barry and Beryl Patten for the Chaplaincy of St Paul, HMS Raleigh, Tor Point Cornwall. Appliqué, machine embroidery and tufting techniques

to cancel out the effect of foreshortening, which would make it appear to be falling out of the banner. The width is often determined by the cross bar of the banner-pole. (An individually designed pole with up-to-date top and end fitings is an advantage.)

Method for making-up
Appliqué, laidwork, inlay and any other embroidery giving a broad effect is most

suitable. Contrast can be introduced by the addition of some machine embroidery. As a banner may from time to time have to be rolled up (for this keep the embroidery outside), when it is transported, it should be practical. Amateurs often produce most interesting and individual work, but the result may be marred by puckering or by poor making-up.

Should orphreys be required, these may either be attached whilst the embroidery is still in the frame, or they can be stitched on with the work laid on flatly.

The selvedge way of the fabric must run down the length of the banner.

1 Before removing from the frame, press over the back of the embroidery with a warm (not hot) iron. Paste the ends on

90 Banner (76 cm×102 cm) by Jacquie Binns for St Mark's Episcopal Church, Washington DC

the reverse side of the work, taking care that no dampness penetrates to the front.

2 Mark round for the outside shape, and put a light tack (using sewing silk) down the centre and another across. (When, if absolutely necessary, due to puckering, the backing has to be cut, it is taken away as near to the work as possible. This would be done before putting in the tacks.)

3 Select the material for interlining, dowlas (when procurable), deck chair canvas, cotton duck, tailors' canvas, heavy holland or unbleached calico, and for weighty works, sailcloth. A good material should not need shrinking, but if it is decided to do so it is framed-up for the operation.

4 Cut the interlining very slightly smaller (about 2 mm) than the actual size of the banner. Mark centres, as for the front.

5 Having removed the embroidery from the frame, cut, leaving about 2.5 cm turnings all round. Spread out on a clean surface, face down. Put the interlining on the back, matching up the centres, pinning (using needles as they mark less) or keeping in place with lead weights. It can be tacked down the centre, but with a thick interlining this is impracticable (*91A*).

6 Turn over the edges on to the interlining, cutting diagonally across or snipping into corners (*91A, C, D*). (The treatment for convex and concave curves is also shown.)

7 Arrange the corners, pin the edges, turn the work over, hold it up, look to see that the front is neither too tight nor too loose, remedy any defects. (With a large banner it is advisable to do the top first, then the sides and lastly the bottom.) Tack the turnings and catch-stitch or herringbone to the back of the interlining, in the order previously mentioned (*91B*). Lightly press the edges on the wrong side (but not for velvet). When the embroidery is heavy it may need to be caught through from the back of the

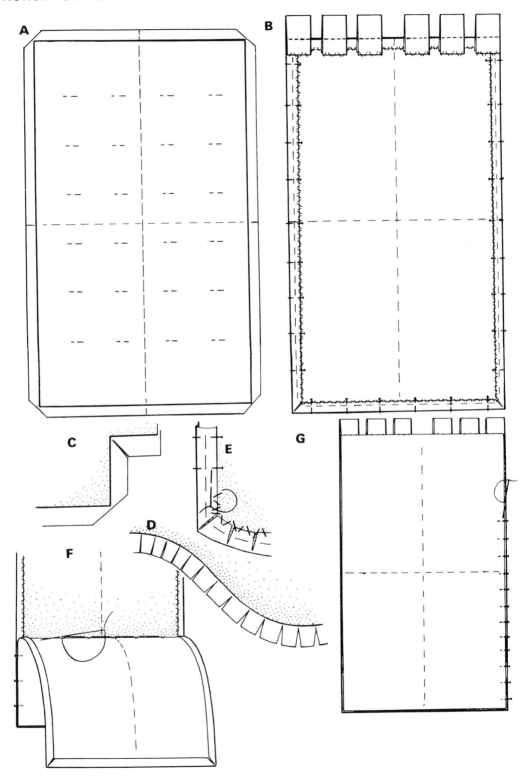

91 Making up a banner

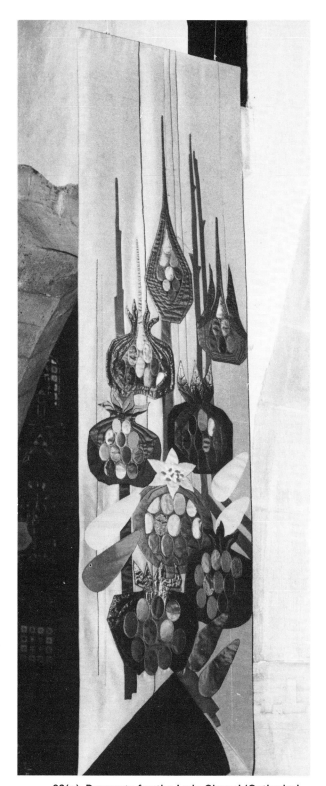

92(b) Designed by Sylvia Green, worked by
Mary Brooks

92(a) Pennants for the Lady Chapel 'Cathedral
of the Forest' Newland, Gloucestershire.
Designed and worked by Beryl Dean

interlining at intervals with tiny stitches on the front and long ones across the back.

8 Prepare the strips (called sleeves) which will form the loops. There should be an equal number, arranged at regular intervals, leaving a space in the centre wide enough for the suspender fitment. An average width for the interlining might be 7.6 cm wide and 10 to 16.5 cm long, plus 2.5 cm turnings at either end; these would be covered according to the method given, and lined with self or a contrasting colour. The loops are then firmly attached to the top edge (*91B*).

Some more ingenious method for fixing the banner to the crossbar of the pole may be thought out, bearing in mind the weight and the fact that it must hang slightly outwards.

(If there is a fringe, it may be sewn on to the interlining or on the front, with the heading showing.)

9 Cut the lining with 12 mm turnings. In theory these edges are turned in and tacked; a centre is marked down and across; it is pinned, then tacked in place, after matching up the centres, and the edges slip-stitched. But in practice the actual size is marked, the centre is put to the centre of the interlining, and it is smoothed outwards from the centre. Then, starting at the top edge, it is turned in and pinned; this allows for adjustment as the work proceeds, the bottom being done last. It can be tacked but this is not really advisable. Slip-stitch the edge (*91G*). Top edge first then downwards, pulling a little tightly out from the centre. The edge of the lining may be a fraction inside the edge of the banner, especially if it is of a contrasting colour. A loop should be sewn on the back and about two-thirds of the way down. This goes round the pole and prevents it hanging too far from it.

Suppose a lining is to cover a very large area or is unsuitable because it is 'floppy', then put the centre to the centre of the interlining, fold back the lining and loosely catch it with a matching thread, using a tiny stitch when penetrating the material or lining and a long one across the interlining (*15 and 91F*), commencing and finishing within about 7.6 cm of the edge; this is repeated at intervals of about 23 cm over the whole surface. The outside edges are then turned in and slip-stitched.

ALTAR FRONTALS

With the interest now centred upon the nave altar, many remarkable Laudian frontals have been produced. From the examples shown it is evident that designers have been stimulated by the challenge and have created embroideries of profundity and great imagination, on a scale to dominate the interior of the cathedral or church.

Few altar cloths being made today have a frontlet or superfrontal.

The colour conforms to the liturgical colour for the season or day.

Material

Many fabrics are suitable, provided that they are not too light in weight, although an interlining could be used. All sorts of interesting weaves and furnishing materials are suitable. Tubular braids, cords, chenille, together with appliqué, and many different contrasting surfaces, all contribute to the embroidery upon the frontal, whether it is done entirely by hand or has machine embroidery as a part of the decoration. Spraying, painting and dyeing can also be included.

Where possible there is a frontal in the colour for each season; otherwise the use of three may be adopted; a best 'white', a ferial of mixed colour, and a Lenten frontal, preferably of unbleached linen. The amount of material required will depend upon the disposition of the seams, which in their turn depend upon the design. Many materials can be used with the selvedge

93 Festal frontal designed by Jane Lemon, the Sarum Group, for Salisbury Cathedral. The design depicts the element water – water of baptism, birth and re-birth. The fragmented cross is shown with water flowing over and through it, and gives another interpretation to the design in the form of grace flowing from the Cross, in all directions to all people

Below

94 All-seasons high altar frontal designed by Jane Lemon, The Sarum Group, for Salisbury Cathedral. 'The Energy' frontal depicts the element air, showing the energy needed today in order to get through the difficulties and lead a full Christian life

95(a) Altar frontal designed and worked by Sylvia Green for St Michael's Church, Highgate, London

grain going across the width of the altar, therefore, for a mounted frontal it is without joins. Otherwise, according to the width of the fabric and size of the altar there may be a centre seam or one towards each side; or more according to the design and method of working.

Measurements
The average height of an altar is 99 cm, the width varies but is usually anything from 1.83 to 3 m or more. If there is a frontlet it should not be more than 15 cm in depth. When cutting, allow generous turnings.

Method
To deal firstly (as it is straightforward) with a frontal which is to be mounted upon a stretcher.

Framing-up or dressing the embroidery frame
Because of the size, there are many problems confronting the amateur. These practical considerations have to be thought out in relation to each other, and to the particular circumstances. For example, before deciding the position of the seams (if any), the design, the sizes of frames available, and whether or not the joins shall be stitched before or after the embroidery is

worked, are factors which must also be determined. It is usually advisable to shrink the material for the backing before use.

The following are possible options:

1 The designer-craftswoman who likes to create as she goes along, may prefer to have a frame large enough to take the backing for the whole frontal (if this is practicable); the advantage being that, as she works, she is looking at it as it will be seen when in use, and she can see most of it all the time.

(a) Join the backing of holland or calico, having cut off the selvedges; material always hangs better with the selvedge grain running downwards, both for the backing and actual fabric. But it may be decided that the advantages of having no seams outweigh this, and so the materials are planned with the selvedge grain running across the width.

(b) Cut off the selvedges, match up the pattern (if any), stitch and press open the seams (if any) in the fabric of the frontal, then mark the centre of each side.

(c) Frame-up the backing, marking the centres of all sides, and apply the fabrics as shown in *figures (127, 128)*. This of course necessitates side-arms long enough to take at least 99 cm,

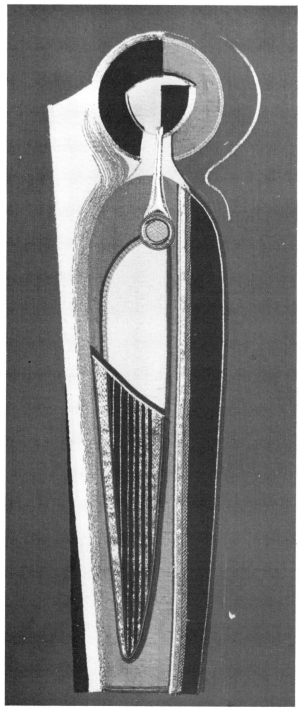

95(b) Detail

plus turnings. (It is convenient to have a shorter pair for use when part of the fabric is rolled in.)

(d) Whilst fully rolled out, the design would be painted on or marked out or drawn on free-hand. Then, if the fabric is light or delicate insert strips of some soft stuff such as cotton blanket or domette attaching it along the webbing. This protects the fabric.

(e) Next, roll in the top and bottom around the rollers, leaving enough exposed to enable the centre section to be worked conveniently; this must be completed at this stage as it is not possible to stretch and stitch further than about 33 cm. Then the frame is gradually unrolled as the work is completed.

More conveniently, the frontal is framed up so that its width (being the longest measurement) is wound round the rollers and as it is completed more is then unrolled. This means that all the embroidery is worked sideways-on, and the whole is not seen until the end.

2 If practicable the frontal can be worked in two or three (or more) sections, each being completed separately, with long threads or lengths of braid left for those lines which cross into the next section. When all have been finished, the joins are stitched (sometimes the two side pieces can be joined to the centre section while it is still in the frame). The loose ends can then be stitched down over the join to complete the design.

3 (a) When the design is confined to a centralised area, frame-up enough backing for this area.

(b) Stitch and press the seams of the frontal fabric. The whole thing can be pinned out for the design to be transferred at this stage or this may be done after the framing-up.

(c) After marking the centres down and across put the fabric in position upon the backing, matching up the centres. This method is similar to that described for a chasuble, *figure 128*. The surplus fabric having been folded over some soft padding, lies on the frame whilst the embroidery is worked.

(d) When completed, the backing is usually cut away close to the stitching.

4 The easiest and most convenient way to set about planning the working of a frontal, especially when it is being undertaken as a co-operative effort, is to have it designed in panels. Then each can be framed-up and embroidered separately and joined with bands of another colour or seamed together afterwards with some decorative edging which is in keeping with the scheme. All too often braids are chosen which, although charming, are complete in themselves, and are out of character with the design, thus striking a discordant note. This method can be artistically dull when the proportions are uninteresting.

5 Another possibility unlikely to appeal to the creative embroiderers of today, is for the main units of a design to be embroidered separately upon linen, or on to pieces of the frontal fabric stitched to framed-up backing. These are then cut out as closely as possible to the outline and applied to the previously framed-up frontal fabric. To keep each motif in position the pins are stuck in vertically, the embroidered motifs are attached with tiny stitches on the right side and long ones underneath at intervals; the outline is stitched down. Some sort of couching or edging must be devised to cover the cut edge, and this needs to be designed to break the hardness of the lines by the introduction of softening rays, spirals, etc.

6 With the immense possibilities inherent in the embroidery of an altar frontal it is impossible to suggest a formula to meet all contingencies. Ultimately the positioning of the seams and the method of framing-up must depend upon common sense. But one basic principle remains and that is for puckering to be prevented. Commercially, pasting is used, but except for smaller areas, it is probably wiser for the amateur, unless very experienced, not to resort to this process. Another reason is that it spoils the nature of the fabric, detracting from its natural beauty. Careful framing-up and preparation will do much to prevent puckering, if it is remembered that the tension and grain of all fabrics applied should correspond.

A typical exception to all this good, but somewhat conservative technical advice, would be a piece of work built up spontaneously. This may entail applying areas of fabric, which may be done when the background is spread out flat on a table, then adding very freely flowing lines and patterning in machine-embroidery; to be followed by some hand stitches such as interlacing and, finally, framed-up for the superimposed embroidery and cords.

Not unnaturally, the embroideress of today may decide to stitch the whole thing, holding it in her hands. And if the background is of a material which can have a final stretching, there is no reason why it should pucker if it has been carefully prepared. This applies for machine embroidery too.

Preparation of embroidery for mounting or making-up

Press the reverse side of the embroidery while still in the frame, stick back the ends. Alternatively, stretch the embroidery if the materials used are suitable. Cut and join the interlining to the exact size. When the selvedge runs across the width and if there is a join, both this and the hem (if there is one), are horizontal. The interlining may be sailcloth, cotton duck, deckchair canvas, and sometimes dowlas.

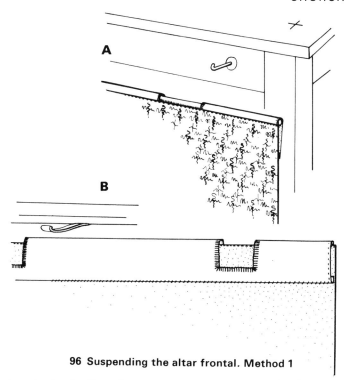

96 Suspending the altar frontal. Method 1

Mark the centres in both directions on interlining and embroidery. Smooth the embroidery out, face down on the table. Put the interlining in position on it, checking up the centres. Turn the edges over on to the interlining and catch-stitch or herringbone-stitch. If may be advisable to lock the face of the frontal right through to the back with tie stitches here and there. Hem in a lining of holland or unbleached calico, unless the lining is cut all in one with the method of suspending the frontal.

Methods of suspending the altar frontal

1 The conventional type of altar frontal can be suspended from an aluminium or copper tube, which is hung upon hooks or lies under the front edge of the altar. *Figure 96A* shows how this is done, seen from the front; it is assumed that this will be covered by the frontlet (mounted in any suitable method). *Figure 96B* shows the method from the back; it is of the false strip of linen or holland measuring the width of the frontal and about 7.6 cm deep. From this are cut three squares, one in the centre of the frontal and one towards each end, the positions corresponding with the hooks on the altar. The edges are neatened with buttonhole stitching. The top edge is stitched to the top of the frontal, and the bottom, having been turned in, is hemmed to the lining of the frontal.

When there is no frontlet, the hooks may have to be raised, and the false strip must be set a little below the top of the frontal so that the rod and hooks are hidden. These slight differences do affect the measurements and so must be taken into account right from the beginning.

2 For this method the top of the altar frontal is attached (very neatly if there is no frontlet) to the edge of the linen covering the top of the altar and hanging down at the back, which is finished with a 5 cm hem, left open at the ends. Through this is slipped a black japanned conduit rod; the weight keeps the frontal in position (*97A*).

The diagram shows the linen cut long enough to form the lining to the frontal, which would be sewn to it all round.

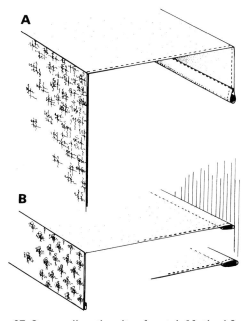

97 Suspending the altar frontal. Method 2

98 Suspending the altar frontal. Method 3

(This would replace the usual lining.) A frontlet can also be attached by this method, but the rod must not be too heavy.

3 *Figure 97B* shows an adaptation of the same method for an altar which is flush with the reredos or wall; here, the rod must be flat. In the diagram the frontlet has been made up in the same way as an apparel and is stitched on to the linen all round. A frontal can be suspended in the same way, whether or not it has a frontal permanently stitched to it.

4 The frontlet in *figure 98A* would be suspended in a similar way, but lead weights are inserted in the hem which must be stitched up at the ends. This is also suitable for a frontal, with or without frontlet attached permanently to it.

5 A further method of suspending a frontal and/or frontlet is to make a linen cover for the top of the altar, allowing

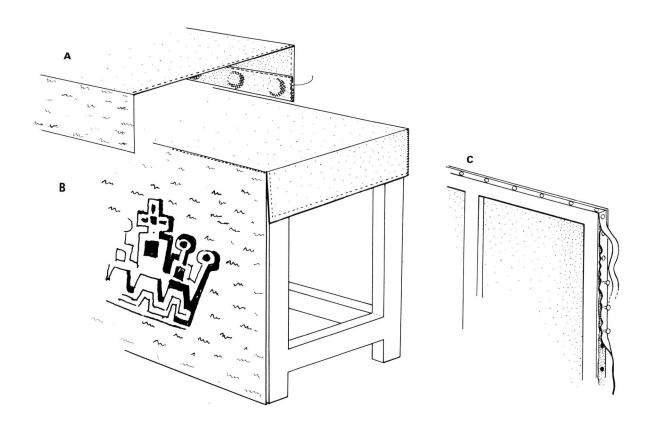

for the two short sides and the back to overhang about 18 cm. Cut away the surplus at the corners so that they fit, overcast them and turn up and stitch the hem. Stitch the frontal to the front edge (*98A*).

6 Another way of mounting a frontal, although seldom advocated now, is nevertheless the most satisfactory to the embroideress. For this a wooden stretcher or frame is made so that it will slip under, or be fixed in front of, the edge of the altar. It is first covered with unbleached calico, which is tacked in place, and over this is stretched the embroidery, the centres being matched up. First the top and bottom, then the sides are bent over and lightly tacked to the frame. Until the whole has been adjusted do not drive home the tacks or nails. Neaten the edges with tape which is also tacked down (*98C*). Or, the turnings can be taken over to the back of the stretcher, then neatened with tape.

THE ALTAR CLOTH FOR A FREE-STANDING ALTAR

Where the altar is free standing and is visible on both sides, it either has a throw-over frontal (or a frontal back and front). This has its own particular dignity, and is a reversion to the older form of pall. It is a rectangle and measures the length and depth of the altar plus twice the height along and across; allow for the hem width. The width and design of the fabric will determine the direction and position of the seams.

All the problems for framing-up for large areas of embroidery are met with when planning hand-stitching the decoration of a Laudian frontal. Yet a frame is an advantage as it helps to overcome puckering, see the section about framing-up (*128*). Few people possess a frame large

99 Detail of white and gold superfrontal, by Judy Barry and Beryl Patten 1980 showing Cornely and Irish machine work

enough to take the whole area to be worked.

Some embroiderers overcome the difficulty of subsequent puckering by mounting the frontal on a stretcher, and putting this in front of the throw-over, arranging the folds at the two front corners so that they hang over the edge of the stretcher, and the front edge of the frontal is put to the top of the stretcher. The width of the throw-over is narrower by the height of the altar.

Making a throw-over or Laudian frontal

If it is decided that the seams shall run along the length of the altar, it is advisable to plan that they correspond with the edges of the altar.

The lining should be sateen, and these seams would be in the same position, as this makes it much easier for locking the turnings together.

The amount of material required is three times the length of the altar + twice its height from the ground + twice the width of the hems.

The diagram shows the altar cloth spread out and the lining kept in place with weights. There can be more than the two essential rows of locking which keep the lining in place (*102*).

When there is a central area of decoration, it may be more convenient to arrange to have one middle width of fabric measuring from the front floor across the altar to the back + hems.

With the embroidery completed, one or more widths of fabric are then seamed to each side.

If lack of space makes it necessary, the corners may be rounded. Sometimes a strip of furnishing or pelmet buckram is inserted between the hem (about 23 cm wide) and the reverse side of the fabric.

When making a throw-over or pall frontal with its seams running lengthwise, press open the seams after stitching, repeat for the lining.

Turn in the hem, about 8 cm, or, if it is to have buckram, about 11 cm wide. Press, catch-stitch if necessary.

Spread out the altar cloth flatly, face downwards. With the wrong side of the lining to the wrong side of the altar cloth,

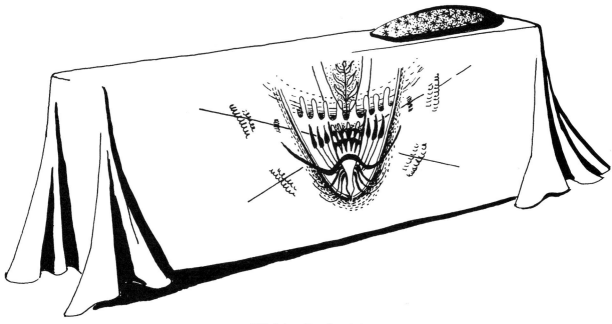

100 A Laudian frontal

101 Frontal for the nave altar, Westminster Abbey, designed by Belinda Scarlett. Detail shown in figure 145

Fine gold gauze, shot silks and organzas, various gold fabrics, many dyed, are used to appliqué the design which is worked on a linen ground Inspiration 'Little Gidding' from *Four Quartets*, by T S Eliot

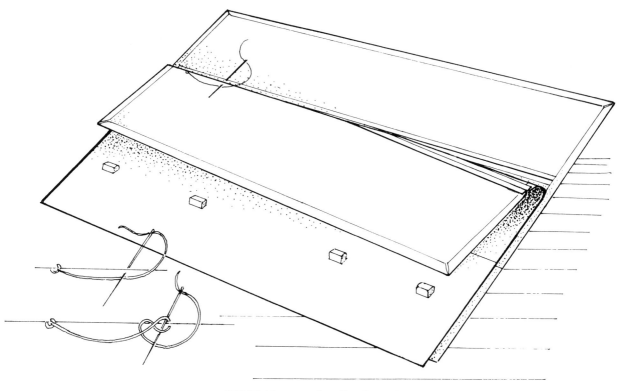

102 Making up a Laudian frontal

spread out the lining, checking that the seams are exactly over each other. (The hem of the frontal would have been pressed up.) Put weights to keep the lining in place, and fold back the lining as shown in *figure 102*.

Lock the edge of the fold with tiny stitches to the reverse side of the frontal, the stitches are about 6 cm apart.

When complete move the fold over, smooth out, and stitch the second seam. This is repeated if more rows are necessary.

Turn in the hem of the lining and slip-stitch on hem.

Shaping of a frontal by means of pleats or gathering is not advisable.

Now seldom seen is an altar according to the English tradition. *Figure 103* shows an altar frontal with frontlet designed as a counter-change. It will be noticed that the conventional fringes on both have been omitted. The riddel-posts bear sconces with tapers. The riddels and the dorsal hangings

are laced with cords to which rings have been attached; these are slipped on to the rods when the hangings are changed according to the season. Where there is a reredos the rods or brackets which support the riddels are fastened to the wall on either side.

On the altar there is a cushion for the Book.

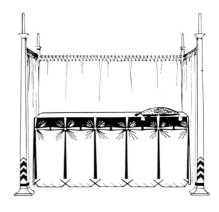

103 The English altar

The Tabernacle Veil

The shape of the veil depends upon the individual tabernacle, which it usually covers. Generally there is a central opening in the veil.

Design

A suitable symbol or symbols, monogram, etc, can be embroidered on either side of the opening, but this should not be stiff as it would prevent the folds falling softly. A simple decorative finish to the hem is an alternative to the inevitable machine-made fringe.

Material

Usually, a soft, fairly thin silk. The colour is generally changed according to the festival or season. Thin Jap silk is suitable for lining.

Measurements

These vary according to the type of tabernacle and shape of veil.

Method 1 for the complete circle (*figure 104 A*)

The radius is determined by the height of the tabernacle taken from its base to the bottom of the cross at the top, plus the width of the hem. Cut a small circle from the centre; nick the turning around it, turn over to the back and neaten with a cross-cut facing. (If decorative braid is used it may be turned on to the right side, where the braid will neaten the edge; the heading of a fringe will do the same for the outside.) The hem around the outer edge will be narrow and may require little darts so that it will lie flatly, or a shaped or cross-cut facing may be stitched on (*104C*).

When lined, after cutting put the right sides of the silk and lining circles together, spread out flatly. After stitching round the edge and on either side of the opening, it may be possible to pull the whole thing through the centre hole to the right side.

This can then be neatened after the whole has been pressed. For thicker

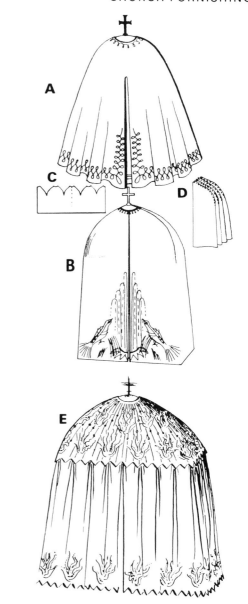

104 The Tabernacle Veil

materials, a section of the edge can be left unstitched for the pulling through.

Method 2 for a shaped, one-piece veil (*figure 104 B*)

The length of the rectangle will equal the measurement round the tabernacle, plus extra for ease, the height equalling the tabernacle from the base of the cross.

Mark the centre of the back, divide into equal sections, pin up shaped darts at each corner to fit the top of the tabernacle.

Mark out and cut, leaving turnings (*104C*). For each corner mark a fold with right sides together, then stitch the darts, tapering off to nothing (as if for a dart in a skirt *104D*), press open. Shape for small centre circle.

If *unlined*, neaten as for the circular veil.

If *lined*, make up the lining in the same way as the outer silk, then put the two together like the circular veil.

Overcast the two sides of the front opening together for a few centimetres at the top, on the inside.

In the sketch another form of tabernacle veil, one with a separate shaped top and curtain, is shown (*104E*). Sometimes the veil takes the form of a curtain in the front of the tabernacle only, the fullness at the top is reduced, and small rings are sewn along; these are threaded on to the little rod.

Another method, when there is a detachable top to the tabernacle, is for the gathered veil to be fixed round the tabernacle, so that the top comes over the heading of the veil.

The inner silk curtains are not embroidered.

105 Detail of an Aumbry Veil by Jacquie Binns for St Alban's Abbey 1987

THE AUMBRY VEIL

This takes the form of a small gathered or pleated curtain, with little rings stitched to the top, which is threaded on to the rod.

THE CIBORIUM VEIL

This is generally a white veil, cut circular. It hangs in very soft folds; if lined it must be very thin. It is made up on the principles already described, although, being smaller, it is more necessary to choose thinner fabrics (*106B*).

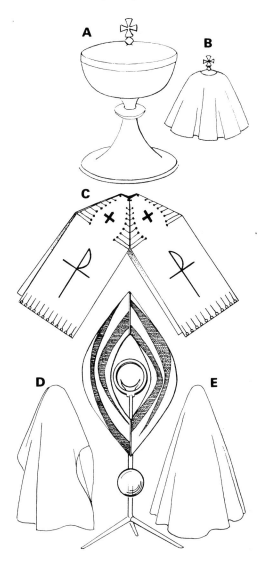

106 The Monstrance Veil

Loops around the circular opening at the top are better avoided.

Still frequently used is the cover (*106C*) made by joining together at the top four embroidered sections. The turnings of each section are folded over an interlining cut to the exact size. After catching these down, a lining is hemmed in.

The Monstrance Veil

This usually measures about twice the height of the Monstrance, and is a strip of soft white silk hemmed around the edges. Or it may be cut as a complete circle, finished with narrow hem (*106D, E*).

The Monstrance sketched (*106F*) is derived from a modern German design.

Funeral Palls

In the USA referred to as Casket palls, they can be very decorative, and are sometimes used also as Easter hangings (*107*). In this country the ceremonial examples can be very interesting, there is a wonderful pall at Rochester Cathedral (now used as a throw-over frontal). But mostly they are restrained though with rich decoration.

It is usually deep black in the Roman Catholic Church, but otherwise may be in any suitable colour.

Design

Generally a cross is gold, either the full

107(a) Casket pall by Beryl Dean for St Mark's Church, Philadelphia, USA

length and width, or terminating with the size of the top of the coffin. For civic or similar use the appropriate coat of arms may be worked in appliqué. There is ample opportunity for a fresh imaginative approach to designing dignified yet more interesting palls.

Materials

A fairly heavy material which will drape well and be practical. Black velvet is not now often used.

Measurements

Vary according to the size of the coffin and purpose. The average coffin is about 183×48 cm $\times 38$ cm deep.

Therefore if the pall is one with its top the size of the coffin, with cut-away corners and a handsome fringe, the width of the fringe will be subtracted from the total depth (*108*). If the pall is a rectangle and intended to drape, it may measure as much as 3.65×2.74 m. The corners can be rounded.

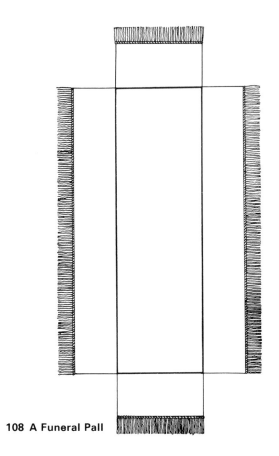

108 A Funeral Pall

107(b) Detail showing patchwork design in white, gold, black, brown and grey

Method

Join the fabric before (sometimes after) the decoration has been applied. Fold the edges over a soft interlining and attach the lining, using the method described for the making-up of a banner. If the seams can coincide with those of the lining, it is much easier to lock together the turnings of both on the inside.

THE PULPIT FALL OR HANGING

Pulpit falls are interesting to design as there is plenty of latitude design-wise and as colour. If there is a fall for each season the design and fabric will link up with that of the other furnishings.

109 Pulpit fall by Beryl Dean for the ancient church of St Mary East Guldeford, Nr Rye, Sussex. Mainly laidwork combined with layers of net

Material

Conventionally silk, but as there is an inter-lining almost any material which is not too bulky. Grosgrain is the perfect weight.

A good quality sateen or any firm material for lining.

Measurements

The width depends upon the size of the stand; the length of the hanging part is in proportion to the width. Generally the fall is longer than it used to be.

Method

Make-up and line the hanging part as for a banner, but do not turn in the edges along the top; put a tacking to keep them together.

Cut a piece of firm strawboard or thin hardboard to the size of the stand and a piece of thinner card to the same size.

Cover the top one either in the fabric or the lining, sticking the turnings over or lacing them as for the burse (30); cover the thinner piece which forms the lining in the same way.

Place the two rectangles together wrong sides facing, pin. One of several ways of securing the pulpit fall to the stand is to have a piece of wide elastic cut to the width plus turnings. Put the elastic across the thinner lining piece (110A) which forms the underside (although usually across the centre, the position needs to be adjusted in relation to the stand), tuck the turnings in between the two boards and stick them to the inside (110B).

Replace the pins, keeping the boards together; overcast around three sides.

With centre to centre tuck the top edge of the hanging part in between the open fourth side of the boards. Slip-stitch along (a curved needle may be useful) (110B).

Turn over and overcast or slip-stitch the lining to the underside of the board.

Other falls are made on the same principle.

Alternatively, it may be considered an advantage when changing the fall and

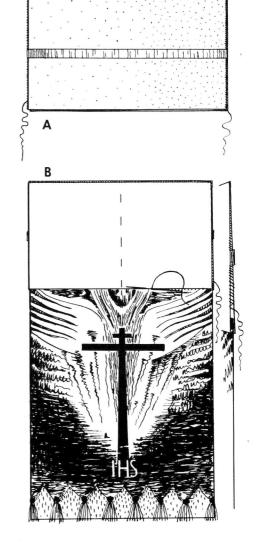

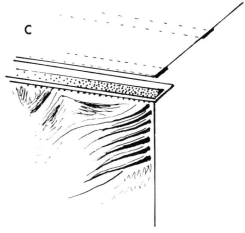

110 Making-up a Pulpit Fall or hanging

when making-up if a narrow strip of *Velcro* is attached across the edge of the underside of the board, and wider turnings are left at the top of the hanging, the edge being neatened and a strip of *Velcro* put along the upper edge as shown at *110C*. This means that one board can be kept permanently in place, just the falls being changed.

Alms Bags

Design

A suitable embroidered unit on the front or an all-over pattern developed from the material. The shape must be functional and with thought it can also be original.

Material

This must be strong, but not too thick or the turnings will be bulky; nor should it be too light in colour. Many furnishing fabrics are excellent as some have woven patterns which can be embellished with simple stitchery, which is an advantage as alms bags need frequent renewal. Canvas work can be used if it is very fine and stitched in silk or stranded cotton.

Method

1 Make a pattern for the back, and for the pocket piece which is a little wider across the pocket mouth.
2 Put the pattern pieces upon the material, seeing that the selvedge grain is running down. Mark out two pieces for the back and one for the pocket piece. Mark in the centre lines and the positions for attaching the pocket piece.

   Cut, allowing 1.5 cm turnings; cut across the corners and clip at intervals along convex curves, snip for concave curves.

   Repeat for the pocket piece.
3 Cut one piece of lining, allowing turnings, for the pocket piece, using polonaise, glazed cotton, sateen or chamois leather; for the latter, no turnings need be allowed as it is hemmed at the edges. Sometimes chamois is joined to the inside

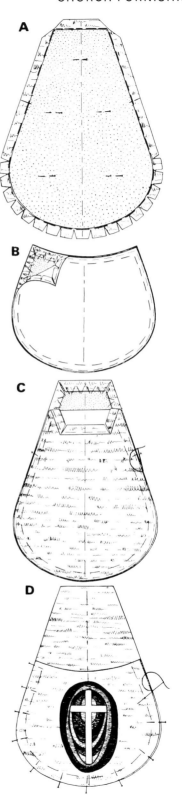

111 Making-up alms bags

of the backpiece, about half-way down.

4 Exactly to the pattern (grain running down), cut the back and front in interlining (*111*), ie dowlas, holland, etc.

5 Pin interlinings in place, tack.

6 Fold over the turnings and lightly catch-stitch (*111B*). Press these edges on the wrong side.

7 Taking the lining pieces fold down the turnings, slightly inside the pattern line, and tack. Pin into position and tack.

8 Slip-stitch a hem round the edges; press (*111C*).

9 Putting centre to centre, and matching up the position at each side of the pocket mouth, pin (*111D*), and tack the pocket piece into position. (This will not lie flatly, if it has been made a little large.) Securing the ends of the pocket mouth very strongly, slip-stitch all round; or alternatively overcast, but this will necessitate a cord as a covering. Always sew into a cord (not over it); start by tucking the end in between the top of the pocket mouth and the back, stitch, then take the cord across the top of the pocket mouth (if this is preferred), then round the edge; or simply round the edge, poking the end down inside the pocket and stitching it invisibly.

Collecting bags with metal fittings

There is scope for well-designed up-to-date fittings. Use strong, practical outer fabric for general purposes. First bind the metal with material; this prevents wear upon the outer fabric.

Cut out the lining pieces in chamois leather, letting the top come to the edge of the metal.

Stitch together round the sides and base.

Cut two rectangles from the interlining and two from the outer fabric; each measuring slightly less than half the circumference of the oval at the top and about 3 cm, allow turnings on the outer fabrics. Fold these turnings over the interlining and catch-stitch. Overcast these two pieces on the wrong side, to the top of the chamois

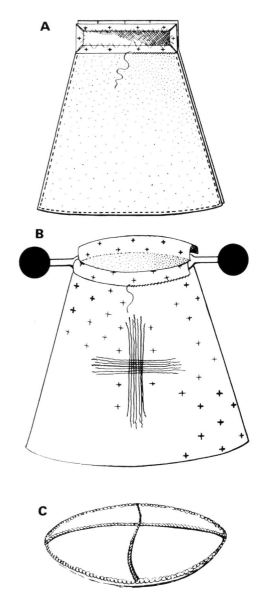

112 Making-up alms bags with metal fittings

bag (*112A*). If the embroidery has been worked with a backing, this can be left in, but cut down to the seam line. Cut out the front and back pieces from the fabric for the outer bag, allowing turnings; seam together down the sides. (To add to the capacity a stiffened oval base can be sewn in), otherwise the bottom edges are joined together. Snip off the turnings at the corners, press the seams open, then turn it out.

Put the chamois lining inside, invisibly catch them together along the top of the chamois.

Then fold the two rectangular pieces over the metal fitting and neatly but strongly hem them down; this can be neatened with couching or a cord (*112B*). Alternatively the bag can be made and lined, but without the two pieces. The top is strengthened and neatened, eyelet holes are either worked at irregular intervals or put in with an eyelleting tool. Then the bag is laced to the fitting with a decorative cord.

There are many other shapes and methods.

When alms basins, trenchers or bowls are used, they are often lined with a detachable circle of felt which has cord stitched either round the edge or underneath, but crossing the circle to facilitate the handling when it is picked up prior to the contents being emptied into the large alms dish (*112C*).

(If a curve would improve the shape, it is quite easy to hold a square of felt over the bottom of another bowl or soup plate, keeping it in the steam from a kettle until it shrinks into shape, then remove and cut to size, and sew on the cord.)

Sometimes the cord is sewn in four loops round the edge, instead of across the circle of felt.

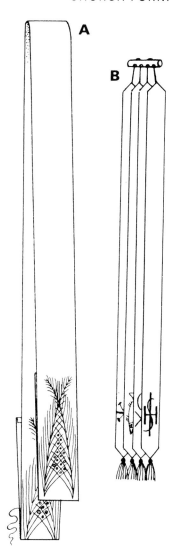

113 Book and Missal markers

BOOK AND MISSAL MARKERS

Design

The embroidery should be confined to that part of the marker which hangs below the book.

Material

If ribbon is used it must not be hard. To avoid damaging the pages a soft fabric is preferable.

Measurements

Take the total of the length of the volume, the projection at the top and the overhang at the bottom.

Double either the length or width, plus turnings, for a marker made of material.

Method

1 Cut twice the usual length plus enough at each end to fold over and hem this down for neatening the back of the embroidery (*113A*). Trace the design on the right side, placing it about 10 cm up from the end, and on the reverse side repeat for the other end. This type of marker is folded over at the top. A single marker is usually preferred.

2 When material is used the marker is made up in the same way as a stole, but without the interlining.
3 Four markers can be attached to a head-piece (*113B*). Fringes and tassels, if not out of scale, give weight to the bottom.

Missal Stand Covers

These too are made in the liturgical colours; the method is similar to that for making the chalice veil. The size varies; some stand covers are stiffened and have braid across the corners to keep them in place. Fringe is not now used as a finish.

Kneelers, Hassocks, etc.

Design
In new churches, when the embroidery is to be commenced before the completion of the building, the architect's scheme for the interior should be known, and his advice sought in relation to colour, design, etc.

Canvas work (tapestry is a misnomer, true tapestry being woven), is the method most suitable for the various kneelers, as it is strong, and, when worked with wool, will soil less easily. Fairly large-scale designs are generally more effective than over-elaboration and small detail. Pattern which

114(a)(b) Kneelers, Phoenix and Dove, for the Lady Chapel 'The Cathedral of the Forest' Newland, Gloucestershire by Sylvia Green worked by Gladys Hope and Carol Douglass

grows out of the characteristics of the decorative stitches is usually preferable to pictoral representations.

Materials

Single canvas (buff is stronger than white) is recommended for most purposes; it is obtainable in several widths and a varying spacing of the threads. The choice depends upon the scale of the design. Double canvas is good for tent and cross stitch. Hemp canvas may be preferred for work which is to be embroidered in the hand.

Crewel wool (two or three strands), tapestry wool (a single strand) and French or Medici wool (three strands) are used, also tapestry needles.

Upholstery materials are discussed in connection with making-up.

Measurements

The smallest kneeler is 23×30 cm $\times 5$ or 7.6 cm. Hassocks may be deeper and a little larger. Sanctuary hassocks are generally considerably deeper and may be somewhat larger; the length, and, to some extent, the width of the communion rail kneelers must depend upon the individual requirements of each church.

When cushions or alms bags are worked in fine canvas work (using stranded cotton), the usual measurements, etc, apply.

Method

When cutting the rectangle of canvas, allow for the depth of the sides, plus turnings; at each corner a square measuring the depth of the sides is left unworked; this forms the shaping when it is later seamed up.

115(a) Choir stall cushion in canvas embroidery depicting the symbol of St Mark for St Michael's Church, Highgate. Designed by Sylvia Green and embroidered by Mary Hall

115(b) Sedilia cushion in canvas embroidery designed by Sylvia Green and embroidered by Mary Hall for St Michael's Church, Highgate. Worked in shades of gold, purple and red on ground of drab green

When framing-up canvas and other materials, where there is no backing, webbing is strongly sewn down both sides; the bracing strings are taken through this.

Transferring
A design which can be worked out to the counted thread will probably be easier to follow if drawn on graph paper and coloured. It is usually advisable to work outwards from the centre.

For the type of design which has greater freedom of line; ink in or paint the outlines of the drawing or tracing. Put this under the canvas; if this has been framed-up, build it up from underneath (with books), so that the design is in contact with the canvas, then paint in the outline.

Work the pattern first and then fill in the background. Many of the simple groundings, worked as all-over patterns, with perhaps a border, are more satisfactory than sophisticated designs, beyond the capabilities of a beginner. Two are given in *figure 117.1, 2*, others can be created or found on old samplers. When working *figure 117.2*, a long stitch added at the end and made with one thread of stranded cotton, serves to emphasise the outline.

Stitches
For uniformity, make the stitches in the same way throughout. Because it is usual for a frame to be used, the needle is shown entering the material; the small crosses in the diagrams indicate the point at which it will emerge.

Figure 117.3(a) To start, make a knot and take the thread through to the wrong side at least 15 mm from the point where the needle will be brought up for the first stitch. This length of thread lying on the back will be worked in as it is covered, and the knot can then be cut off.

Figure 117.3(b) *Tent* stitch worked in diagonal lines across the canvas may be stronger than when worked in horizontal rows.

Figure 117.3(c) For joining, bring the old thread up, 15 mm away (finish off in the same way). Start the new thread as for the commencement. They will be covered as the work progresses.

Figure 117.3(d) *Cross* stitch or *Gros Point*. The final crossing stitch must always be in the same direction.

Figure 117.3(e) The *Cross Lorraine* is composed of eye stitches.

Figure 117.3(f) The outlines are worked in back stitches. When these are combined to form a grounding, contrasting colours add interest.

Figure 117 D (4) Two-sided *Italian Cross* can be utilised in several different ways. Each stage in the working of the back stitches of which it is composed can be followed from the diagram.

Figure 118.1 *Long-armed Cross* or *Greek* stitch. Commence by bringing the needle up at the point marked by the arrow, then

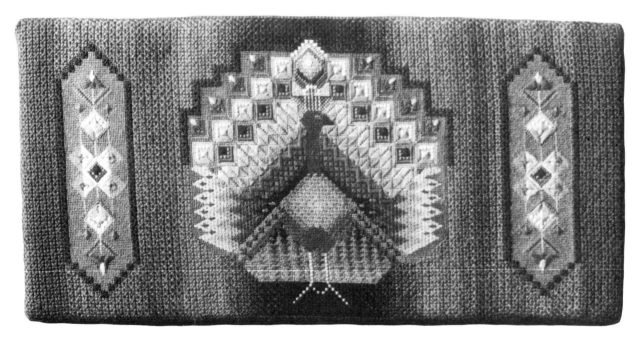

116 Two of a set of kneelers designed by Sylvia
Green for St Michael's Church, Highgate
(a) The 'Bee' worked by Margaret Hill
(b) The 'Peacock' worked by Carol Douglass

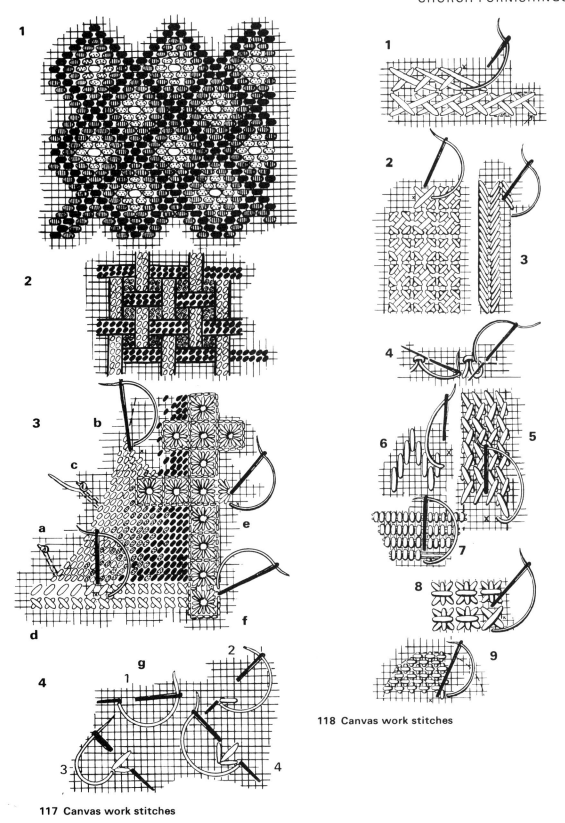

117 Canvas work stitches

118 Canvas work stitches

take the thread over a square of four threads of the canvas, putting the needle through the material, bringing it out four threads back; this thread will then be taken obliquely forward over eight vertical and four horizontal canvas threads and brought out four threads back; this is then repeated and for the next row it is reversed as shown in the diagram. When worked by this method two parallel lines of back stitches are formed on the reverse side.

Figure 118.2 Rice, Crossed Corners or *William and Mary*; this is suitable for large spaces and it has the advantage of covering the ground quickly.

Figure 118.3 Diagonal Satin stitches worked in lines over two vertical and three horizontal threads of the canvas.

Figure 118.4 Single Knotted stitches; one or more of these stitches can be introduced into a piece of work to add interest. They are worked in the same way as a single Maltese stitch. It should be realised that, whereas in the diagram a single thread is illustrated, to be effective, a group of several strands would in reality be used; when the loops are cut little tassels are formed. The needle is shown in position for the first stages of a second stitch, and the one on the right shows the completion.

Figure 118.5 Plaited Gobelin; the stitches all face in the same direction for one row and in the opposite way for the next.

Figure 118.6 Florentine; this is one of the most characteristic of the canvas stitches, and must be worked over an even number of threads.

Figure 118.7 Upright Gobelin; though this is a useful stitch it does not always completely cover the canvas. This disadvantage can be obviated by laying a self-coloured thread along the line and working over it.

Figure 118.8 Smyrna or *Double-cross* stitch; this is a diagonal cross with a straight cross worked over it. An attractive variation can be obtained by using a single strand of crewel wool worked over two instead of four threads; two colours alter-

nating heighten the effect.

Figure 118.9 Straight or *Upright Cross*; as the name implies, the stitches are taken vertically and crossed horizontally over two threads of canvas. It is usually found more satisfactory to complete each stitch before proceeding to the next (as shown in the diagram) – though this gives one of the most delightful textures, it does take longer to work.

Figure 119 A Encroaching Gobelin. From the enlarged detail it will be seen that the stitches should slant across, one vertical and four or five horizontal threads. The stitches of each succeeding row encroach between those of the previous one. The resultant smooth surface acts as a foil to the more ornamental texture.

Figure 119 B Another variation of *Upright Gobelin*. Here, a thread is laid along the line and the stitches are worked over it. The canvas is less likely to show, and there is the advantage of a ridge which forms an interesting texture.

Figure 119 C This variation of *Upright Gobelin* may not cover the canvas, but this disadvantage will be less evident if the canvas is painted before working.

Figure 119 D Hungarian stitch. This is very adaptable; by changing the colours, decorative patterns can be formed.

Figure 119 E Mosaic stitch. The smallness of the scale renders it useful for intricate shapes.

Stretching

When a piece of canvas work is finished, it should be kept in the frame, but unrolled and straightened up if necessary. It should then be turned with the reverse side upwards, and thoroughly dampened with a sponge and water, and allowed to dry off for about twenty-four hours.

If, however, it has been worked in the hand, or it is out of shape, it is necessary to pin or nail the work out upon a wooden surface. Place the embroidery face upwards with one straight selvedge side to the edge of the broad, stretch it, and pin or nail out the second edge at right angles to the first. Do the same with the third and fourth sides; these will require more pulling to get the shape accurate. *Figure 121A* shows this process.

Thoroughly dampen with a sponge and water, being sure to dab rather than rub; the latter would cause the wool to fluff up. Allow to dry for about twenty-four hours.

The threads should be tested first and if the colour is likely to run, a cloth should be placed underneath as this absorbs the surplus dye and moisture.

This process is used for any embroidery worked on fabric which will not be harmed by the damping; for work on linen the embroidery is put face down. For light materials sometimes it is sufficient to pin out over damp clean blotting-paper or cloth.

Making-up a kneeler worked in one piece

To make-up a kneeler which has been worked in one piece, after stretching, cut the canvas, leaving 2 cm turning all round (*121B*). Stitch the corner seams, press flatly and turn out.

For hanging up the kneeler, make a loop, pass this through a ring, and firmly attach it in the centre of one short side.

To make up a kneeler with separate sides of contrasting colour or material, join these at the corners, then prepare and stitch in the piping (*122*). After matching up the corners of the top with the corners of the sides, stitch together.

There are *several possible fillings* from which to choose, for each the method is slightly different.

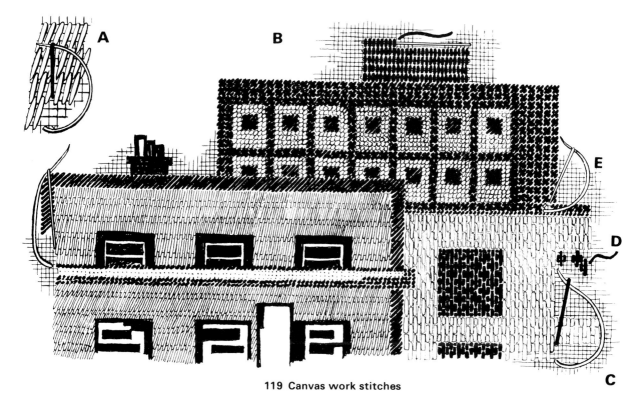

119 Canvas work stitches

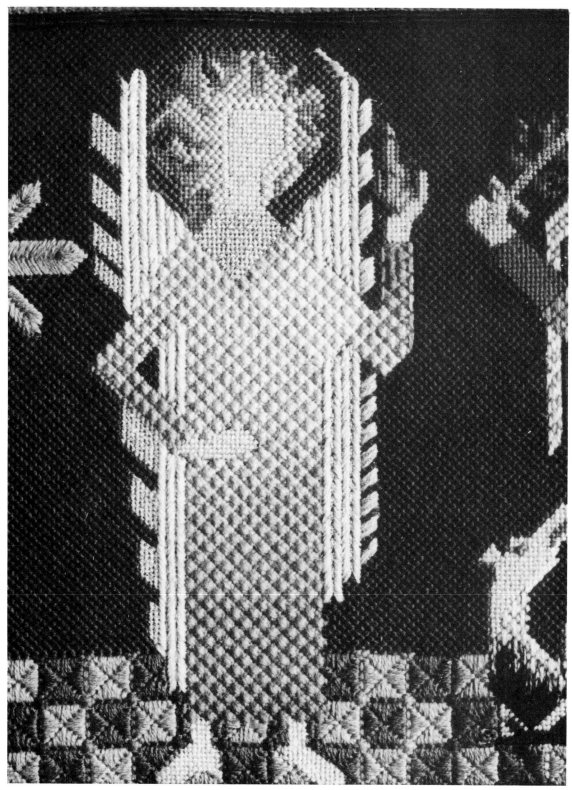

120 Detail from cushion for St Michael's
Church, Highgate, London, by Sylvia Green

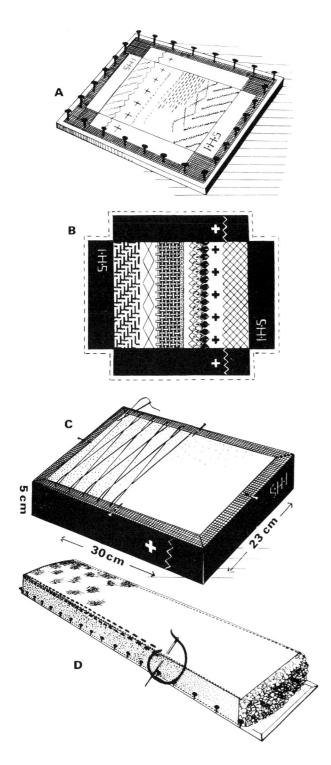

121 Making-up kneelers

1 *Rubber latex.* This needs to be thicker than the depth of the kneeler; so that it can be compressed, it can be cut with very sharp scissors. Cover with calico and always add several layers of thick carpet felt. The disadvantage is that after being in use for some time, the covering is apt to slip off the edges, even when the corners are stitched through.

2 For *plastic foam*, see list of suppliers, the process is similar, but 7.6 cm or 10 cm of the foam must be compressed to 5 cm. Layers of thinner plastic foam and thick carpet felt are another possibility.

3 Several thicknesses (cut to shape) of *carpet felt* stitched through, but this is rather heavy.

For any of the above methods, the interior is slipped inside the cover, and if necessary some wadding is stuffed into the corners. The turnings of the canvas can be stitched down to the rubber or felt on the underside, or it may be laced across (*121C*). Next, cut a rectangle of black upholsterer's linen (sometimes called bucket-cloth) and press down the turnings, match up the centres and corners with those of sides of the cover, hem this lining all round to neaten the bottom. Sew on a ring for hanging, if this is required.

4 When *plastic foam cuttings*, *rubberised hair*, or *horsehair* is used, the black linen lining for the base is pinned and hemmed to three sides of the cover of the kneeler (for horsehair first put in a thick layer of wadding), then pack in as much stuffing as possible so that it is really very firm, press well into the corners, then pin, closing the fourth side by hemming it to the lining.

To make up a communion rail kneeler, stuffed with horsehair

1 Cut out the top, bottom and sides of the case in hessian, allowing extra for turnings and 2.5 cm extra for every 30 cm of the length.

2 Join this together with outside stitching

on right side, using a sewing machine; leave one end open.

3 Stretch out this case, and nail through the seams of the base (*121D*).

4 Tease out the horsehair, and push into the interior, using a regulator or knitting needle to get it right into the corners.

5 Using fine string threaded into an upholstery needle, stab-stitch along the edges; this helps to keep the shape.

6 With a very long upholsterer's needle and string, stitch right through, from top to bottom and back, pulling it tightly and tying the ends. This is repeated at intervals, keeping one row 5 cm in from the edge. Although the *figure 121D* shows this, it would not be done until the stuffing had been completed and the open end stitched up, and nails and tacks removed. These ties prevent lumps forming in the horsehair.

7 Fill up with wadding the indentations caused by the tying and knotting of the string. Put a thick layer of wadding all over the top to ensure that it is smooth and flat.

8 When the outer covering has been put over the whole kneeler, the upholsterer likes to make the job more rigid by tying through again with string and buttons or tassels, but the designer of an embroidered communion rail kneeler prefers to sacrifice this in the interest of an unbroken surface.

The lining for the bottom is hemmed on.

Kneeling pads

These are made up on the same principle as other kneelers, but omitting the gusset. For these a ring for hanging them is essential. The cover can be of leather, durable fabric or plastic, or it can be in canvas work.

CUSHIONS

Used instead of book-rests or Missal stands, they rest upon the altar and pulpit.

Design

These cushions are usually made of plain material. If there is embroidery it is generally a simple cross. Metal threads are unsuitable as these would scratch the binding.

When the cover is of canvas work, it is important that the design forms an integral part of the whole scheme, especially the colours used. If the cushion does not match the frontal, it should look right with it.

Measurements

Altar or Missal cushions, about 53×30 cm or 41×26 cm. These measurements can be varied according to requirements.

The cushion for the prie-dieu may be larger.

Material

When the cover has to be used for all seasons, velvet (if not shiny) or a soft furnishing fabric or thick silk, such as Thai silk, should be used. A slippery silk is not suitable. A fairly neutral colour is useful. For detachable covers the choice is wider. Sometimes cord is still used to neaten the edge, with tassels at the corners.

Method

From pillow ticking cut two rectangles slightly larger than the finished size plus turnings. (One side may be a fold). Machine stitch or overcast all round leaving about 12.5 cm open in the centre of one side (*122A*). Turn out to the right side.

Tease out plenty of kapok, no lumps should remain. If horsehair and feathers are used, the same applies. (Alternately foam latex can be used, but it is not recommended.) Insert handfuls of the filling, pressing it well into the corners. It needs to be fairly firm but not too full. Then sew up

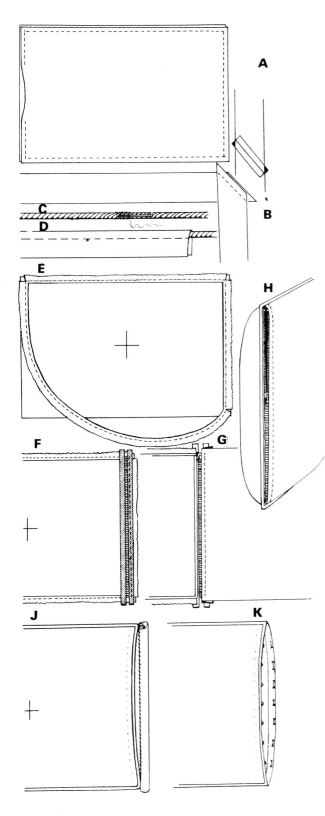

122 Making a cushion cover

the opening. The seams can be soaped to prevent feathers poking through. The cushion for the pulpit is usually a little flatter.

To make the cover, cut out two rectangles plus turnings.

If there is to be a piping, cut a strip on the cross of the material about 3 cm wide. The length is the total measurement of the four sides plus 12 mm for the join.

Seam the join (*122B*), and press the seam open.

Take a length of piping cord; this can either be cut to the exact length, with the two ends brought together with stitches or it can be spliced; for this an extra 12 mm is allowed (*122C*). Then wind a thread round it. Next, fold the strip of material over the cord and run stitch it or machine stitch, using the piping foot (*122D*).

Pin this continuous length to the right side of one rectangle, tack, snip the turnings at the corners, stitch (*122E*).

If the cover is not to be detachable, and whether or not there is a piping, put the two right sides together; stitch round, leaving about 33 cm on the short side open. Press and turn out.

Persuade the interior gently through the opening and well into the corners. Pin the opening and slip-stitch.

When there is a detachable cover in each liturgical colour, the neatest opening is made with a fine dress zip fastener put along the short side, in the seam. With the right side of the zip and the right side of the front rectangle of material facing, place it so that the right-hand tape comes over the stitching line. Stitch along this line (*122F*). (If there is a piping these stitches will come on top of the previous row securing the piping.) Fold the zip back, and invisibly catch the turning of the piping and the tape to the wrong side of the fabric, which can be neatened with bias binding.

Next, take the rectangle of fabric for the back of the cushion; fold and tack back the turning along one short side. Place this over the zip to hide it. To make *figure 122G* clearer, it is not completely covering it, though it should do in practice. Stitch well clear of the zip, keeping the zip almost closed, and with the right sides of the two pieces of fabric together; stitch round the three remaining sides, upon the line of the piping stitches. Open the remainder of the zip and turn out (*122H*).

Method 2

Put the two rectangles together right sides facing. Stitch round three sides.

Fold back the turning on one short side of the front, neaten it by invisibly hemming a facing or bias binding on the reverse side. Cut a strip the length of the short side, and twice the finished width, plus turnings, for a facing.

With the right side of this facing to the right side of the back of the cushion, stitch along the short side. Turn the other edge over to form a lay, and fold it over to the first row of stitches, then hem it (*122J*).

Tuck in the ends, stitch and fold in this facing.

Should hooks and eyes be preferred the hooks are sewn to the front, not allowing the stitches to penetrate, and sew eyes to the facing on the back (*122K*).

But narrow strips of *Velcro*, sewn to the facings would be more satisfactory.

EMBROIDERY AND TECHNICAL METHODS

CREATING THE DESIGN

THE whole concept of embroidery for the church has changed in the years since this book was originally written. Important works of art in this medium have been created for cathedrals and churches throughout the country. Experienced creative embroiderers and designers established in other fields have contributed to an up-to-date lively approach to the subject. Machine embroidery has developed enormously combined with experimentation in other unrelated techniques.

Inviting as the decoration is, this book has to concentrate upon the construction of vestments, soft furnishings and hangings. It is essentially about obtaining a good standard of finish, because it is so important. However excellent is the decoration the effect can be spoiled by unprofessional making-up.

Only briefly considered will be the issues concerning design, as other books (see further reading page 172) deal with the subject. However, the main points in relation to designing for this aspect of embroidery are summarised, and concern the ambient in which these things are seen and used. All important is the architecture, and general colour scheme. For large projects the designer would confer with the architect and others concerned.

Confidence in the designer-embroiderer should lead to her being afforded the latitude to make necessary decisions as she is generally well qualified, having had an art and technical training. But it must depend upon the perception, artistry and practical experience of that person.

The ideal is for the craftswoman also to be the designer; in this way the whole work is conceived as a unity of decoration, including the choice of materials and techniques. With the introduction of a combination of machine and hand embroidery, the ever increasing freedom of line is bringing great changes. To quote Professor Edgar Wind, by 'arresting a work at the point of greatest spontaneity' the vitality is captured.

The rearrangement of the east end of the church, consequent upon the introduction of the free-standing or nave altar means that much thought must be given to preserving the unity of the scheme as a whole.

That it is the job of a professional to advise, cannot be over-emphasised; training and experience form the basis of his judgment. He can visualise the effect of the introduction of additional colour and the tone required to make it show up against the surroundings. Splendidly enthusiastic and well-intentioned amateurs are apt to concentrate upon each individual 'opus', without considering it as part of a whole scheme, and so there results a conflict with the existing character and decoration. It is difficult to add further ornamentation where there are already several styles in the glass, carpeting, banners, and perhaps a

carved and coloured reredos; this is a common enough problem, not only in cathedrals, but in almost all older churches. Those who have the courage to suggest breaking away from the conventional type of design need support and constructive understanding. And, until more good creative designer-craftswomen are sufficiently interested to master the specialised requirements, there is little to suggest to those who want to be put in touch with designers, except perhaps to approach the embroidery instructor at a college or school of art, or technical college, or by getting in touch with the Council for the Care of Churches or the Crafts Centre of Great Britain, or the Embroiderers Guild.

To make a start on designing
In this specialised field it is impossible to

123 Altar cloth designed by Belinda Scarlett for Snape Church, Suffolk:
'God is the still point at the centre.'
Julian of Norwich
The design is worked as a painting onto the entire silk ground: the dyes are sprayed onto the fabric by means of stencils, to build up translucent layers of colour. Other fabrics are then appliquéd in certain areas – for example, the curlew, the reeds, the dove, the shimmer on the surface of the water

think about designing without first considering the context in which the object will be seen or if it is a vestment, that it has to be worn. This will influence the scale.

At the planning stage the scheme should be kept simple and of good proportions. It is more likely to be satisfactory if it depends upon the hang of the garment and its deep folds than on intricate, small details of decoration.

If intimidated by the initial commencement – make a start with your material, perhaps you are excited by the colour, it may be interesting to put another texture with it, keeping it to self-colour, and limiting the amount of decoration but always decide where the emphasis shall be. Alternatively, perhaps the embroidery is to be important. You may, for example, want something symbolic, if so keep it simple

and keep it large! Imagine the seeds and miniature trees, treat them as conventionalised pattern, stick to one idea and develop it. Try arranging the shapes until you arrive at something satisfactory. You can be very inventive as you develop it in terms of stitchery.

The design might be abstract, depending upon an exciting colour scheme and composed of interesting shapes and superimposed linear rhythms. On looking at the illustrations throughout the book, the many variations of design will be observed, and may well spark off imaginative ideas.

There are many levels of achievement. Some people are capable of sketching out their ideas, which, when enlarged, may form the basis of a large composition. It will be noted that the images are treated decoratively, they must not become an

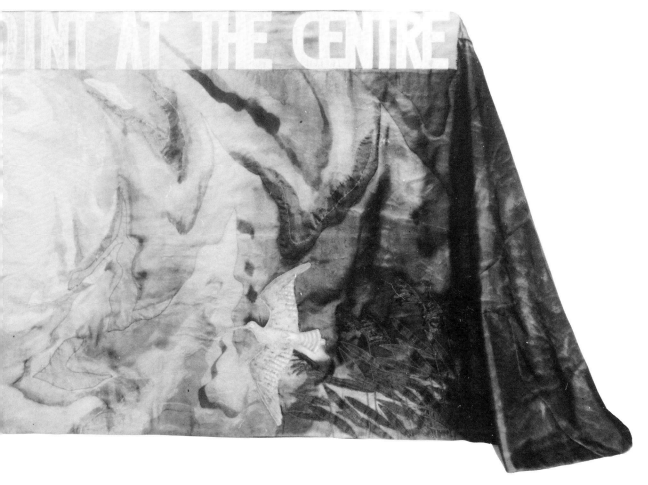

illustration, as this is intended to depict a story.

The immediate concern is with decoration, and for subject matter there is the whole of symbolism to stimulate the imagination. Originally a visual language, these symbols convey a meaning and are capable of decorative interpretation. This need not exclude either formalised figure subjects or geometrical designs.

When starting to design try to capture the mental image of the idea, then arrange the shapes and lines so that there is an overall rhythm running through the composition. A certain repetition of direction in the lines may help (*125*).

Then decide how the interest is to be concentrated in relation to the general shape. For example, in planning the decoration upon a chasuble, decide whether there will be a wide orphrey down the centre of the back and front or a powdering of small units all over. Or, alternatively, if it is to be composed of one or more symbols combined to form a unit, let this be really large; there is always a tendency for the scale to get too small in detail. Another possibility is to embroider an all-over repeating pattern in the yoke space of the chasuble.

Proportion is important in all designing. For instance, if the embroidered area covers one-third or two-thirds of the whole it is more visually satisfying than making it half and half. The centre of interest might be one-third of the distance down from the neck of the chasuble.

Select an original subject for the design, thinking out an interesting interpretation, avoiding the hackneyed which, through over-familiarity, has lost its impact. Much of the sterile and meaningless decoration still being perpetuated is watered-down decadent Baroque in style. A characteristic of present-day design lies in its freedom and movement. The embroiderer has to be sensitive to this and seek to translate the vital and accidental quality of a first sketch.

124 Designing for church embroidery

Simple woven or printed devices decorating the fabric can be developed to form design, the nature of the technique itself adding interest. The designer, seeking inspiration, will surely find it in Byzantine mosaics, ivories and painting, Gothic sculpture, missals, illuminated manuscripts, embroideries (*Opus Anglicanum*) and stained glass; Romanesque enamels, thirteenth-, fourteenth-, and fifteenth-century frescoes and murals, also the illustrated bestiaries.

Look at everyday things as if you have never seen them before, for example, the shadow cast by a fern upon a wooden plank. Might this not suggest an idea (*124*) for a design of palm leaves and shadows falling upon a cross composed of tubular braids sewn down to follow the graining and knotting in the wood? Even the shadow cast by the thickness of the plank

125 Altar cloth designed by Belinda Scarlett for *Lambeth Palace Chapel*:
A combination of methods is used: the dyes are painted directly on to the silk ground. Areas of quilted appliqué are then worked into the design. Inspiration by 'Choruses' from *The Rock* by T S Eliot

would add interest to one side of the cross, interpreted in net or velvet.

Nobody need be afraid to make the effort to design and thereby derive the additional satisfaction of creating. Keep the scheme really simple, it 'tells up' and is much more satisfactory than the over-ambitious plan which requires the knowledge and construction beyond that possessed by the average embroiderer.

Designing an altar frontal, banner or large hanging may be beyond the capabilities of the technically proficient embroiderer. It is preferable that a trained designer who is sympathetic to the medium, should carry it out, as nothing is worse than a figure which is 'out of drawing'.

THE USE OF COLOUR

When planning a colour scheme it is vitally important to look at your collection of materials in the church, and to make a selection in-situ, because the light in each individual building can completely change colours.

The liturgical colours are white or gold, red, green, rose-pink, black or purple, and the 'off-white' of Lenten array. These are not any particular tints or shades. All greens, for instance, are liturgically green. The Eucharistic vestments conform to the colour for the season or day and so, when possible, do the altar frontal, the hangings, etc. For the cope and mitre this is optional.

The colours of many fabrics produced commercially for the purpose are often harsh and very ordinary. Furnishing fabrics are more interesting in this respect. It is always wise to look at a sample in the church, judging it against the surroundings.

When considering the choice of colours it is important to realise the relative tone-values, ie dark, medium and light, and to avoid putting side-by-side similar areas of two different colours of the same tone. For example, olive-green and maroon-red, put together in the same quantity, are unsatisfactory. But to change the dark red to scarlet is instantly an improvement.

Very briefly and generally, the colours used are as follows:

White and/or gold All Saints' Day, Christmas, Feast of the Epiphany, Easter, Ascension, Trinity Sunday, Weddings, etc, and Feasts of Our Lady, etc.

Red Feasts of the Martyrs, Whitsuntide, Feast of the Apostles (ie Martyrs), etc. (Passiontide, deep red; Whitsuntide, bright red.)

Blue or violet in the Church of England, Advent, Lent (first four weeks).

Purple in the Roman Catholic Church, Holy Innocents, Vigils, Advent, Lent (first four weeks), etc.

Red Passiontide. In the Church of England for the remaining Sundays in Lent and Good Friday, altars are bare.

Green Epiphanytide, Season of Trinity to Advent, etc.

Black Funerals, All Souls' Day. In the Roman Catholic Church, Good Friday.

Rose-pink after Trinity and as a general ferial colour. In the Roman Catholic Church, fourth Sunday in Advent and mid-Lent Sunday.

Yellow in the Church of England, Feast of Confessors.

EQUIPMENT

Good strong embroidery frames, known as slate, four-piece or rectangular, with pegs, should be used in preference to the variety which extend by screwing. Old frames, provided that they have not warped, are often more satisfactory. The size is determined by the length of the webbing attached to the roller.

The use of an embroidery frame keeps the work flat and without puckers. They are essential for gold work. However, with this exception, many people prefer the freedom of managing without, as it leaves the worker able to combine machine em-

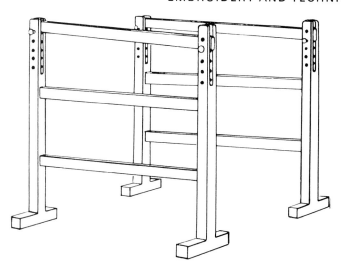

126 Trestles to support embroidery frame

broidery when building up a design spontaneously.

A pair of trestles or stands on which to support the frame, are needed so that both hands are free. For those who undertake large-scale work trestles are a necessity (*126*).

Substitutes can be improvised, but it is an advantage if the top bar can be adjustable.

The usual equipment needed for drawing should include a set square. And some small weights, used during tracing-on and when making-up.

For framing up, use steel pins; a packing needle, large enough to take string; string by the ball or in lengths; reels of strong cotton thread; tape measure; embroidery scissors with good sharp strong points, also a large pair for cutting out. Two thimbles (if used); crewel needles of good make (Nos 8 and 9 are useful sizes), also some sharps for making-up. Chenille needles Nos 18, 20 and 22 are used for taking the ends of the gold thread through to the back. For canvas work, tapestry needles Nos 18, 20 and 22. A stiletto. Working threads are passed through bees-wax to give additional strength. Hammer and nails.

FRAMING-UP
OR
DRESSING THE FRAME

When *couching down* Japanese gold and metal threads, both hands are required for the manipulation, and it is therefore essential to use an embroidery frame. By doing so puckering is avoided; another advantage is that it is possible to view the embroidery as a whole, which enables the balance, colour and emphasis to be considered as the work progresses.

It is usual to have a backing. This can be of evenly woven white or unbleached linen, holland or unbleached calico, a wide and narrower width is obtainable.

The backing should be coarse or fine according to the nature of the work, and is generally thoroughly washed and shrunk before use.

Method

1 Cut the backing to the thread at least 2.5 cm larger than the material to be embroidered. All materials must be cut with the selvedge way running down. This is most important to the finished result; the only excpetion is when it is

artistically justified by the advantage gained in having a pattern or stripe running in the opposite direction.

2 At the top and bottom, fold down 12 mm on to the wrong side, hem down if likely to fray.

3 At both sides fold back a good 12 mm, insert string at edge, pin in place. Stab stitch with a strong thread using a back stitch at intervals (127A).

4 Measure the exact centre of the webbing attached to the rollers or cross-bars of the frame; mark this permanently.

5 Put a tack down the centre of the backing; place this to the centre of the webbing; when in position pin with the pins at right angles to the edge; work outwards. Using very strong thread, overcast, starting at the centre each time and stitching towards the ends. Repeat for the second roller. This is shown in the diagram. (If the work is large a ridge can be avoided by placing the right side of the backing to the right side of the webbing, pinning and doing the overcasting on the wrong side.)

6 Slip the two side pieces (slats) through the slots in the rollers of the frame.

(These flat laths have holes pierced at intervals along their length.)

7 Extend so that the backing is almost taut and insert the four pegs or split-pins into the appropriate holes. Measure for accuracy.

8 Take very strong string of sufficient length and thread this into a packing needle. Lace through the sides of the backing and over the side pieces at about 2.5 cm apart, as in the diagram. Leave about 46 cm (more when some of the material is rolled in), wind round the ends of the frame and tie off.

9 Cut by the thread the piece of material to be used (selvedge running down); tack down the centre using a fine silk thread. (When the whole area is to be covered with embroidery, a fine linen is used.)

10 Place the fabric with the centre directly over the centre line on the backing.

11 Working out from the centre, pin with the head of the pin outside and pointing inwards.

12 Stitch with fairly long straight stitches as at 2 in the diagram; or the piece can be herringbone stitched. Complete the

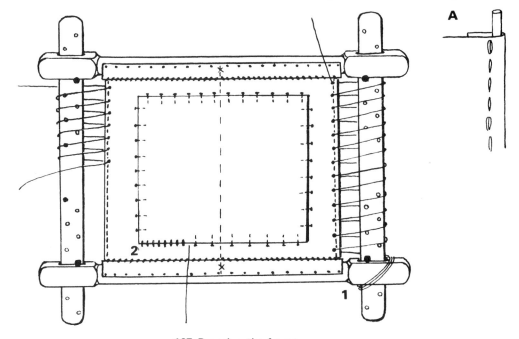

127 Dressing the frame

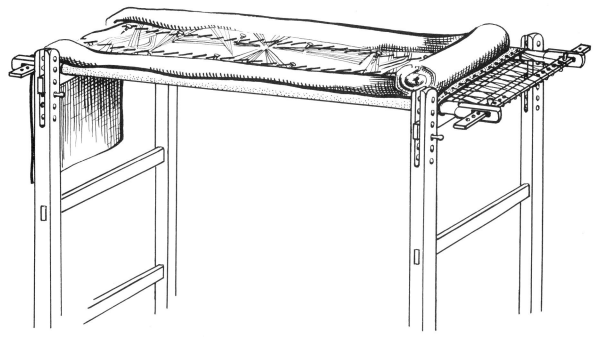

128 Stitching the backing on to the frame

top and bottom, then the two sides.

13 Tighten up the frame and brace up the sides so that it is absolutely taut. It should always be tightened up when it becomes at all slack.

NB *Figure 127* shows a frame set up for a small piece of work such as a burse. For larger pieces, the width of the rollers must measure the width of the backing; longer side-arms are used to take the increased length, and to keep this tight for stitching and painting on to the outer fabric. This completed, the slats are withdrawn, the extra length rolled round one or both rollers, and the shorter sides put in. It is unrolled as the work proceeds.

To frame-up for embroidering isolated decoration upon a larger area of fabric. For this certain difficulties are encountered. The following information may be found helpful.

Method

Most of the problems of framing-up large pieces are encountered in the preparations for embroidering a chasuble, and the fol-lowing suggestions apply equally for copes and frontals, etc.

Determine which seams can be completed before framing-up, stitch them and press open.

Where there are shoulder seams these can usually be joined after the embroidery has been done. (When lines of the embroidery continue over such seams, the stitchery is taken as close as practicable and long threads are left until the end, when they are threaded up, and the stitchery is worked by hand over the seam.)

Paint on the design at this stage or after framing. Having drafted out the pattern, put it on the fabric, selvedge down the length, thread-mark round the outside of the pattern line (not the cutting line).

(As an exception, if the frame is large enough and the material is firm and the embroidery light, the fabric itself can be framed-up. It is marked out, but the fabric must remain a square or rectangle.)

The nature of this type of embroidery makes the use of a frame essential. But if the design is not all-over, or if the whole would be too large to frame-up, the following method is one way of overcoming the difficulty:

I

1 The backing for chasubles is usually washed unbleached calico, thin linen or cambric, etc. Cut this to the size of the embroidered area plus turnings.
2 The backing is stitched into the frame (*128*). It may be more convenient if it is mounted and worked sideways on.
3 Take the fabric to be embroidered (*128*), make the centre correspond with the centre marked on the backing (which is kept fairly slack).
4 Pin, keeping the pins (or needles) all in one direction, smoothing the fabric out from the centre, keeping the tension of both materials the same. Tack in lines of zigzag tacking all over. Tighten up the frame by moving outwards the pegs and bracing up the string.
5 Fold the surplus material over something soft, down the length, then across. (Try not to lean on this whilst working, because deep creases will not always come out afterwards.)

As each part is completed, more backing is unrolled on one or both sides, then the fabric too is unrolled, pinned up and tacked. It is impossible to reach more than about 33 cm for stitching.

II

It is, of course, much easier to work orphreys or separate units upon linen; then, cutting this away close to the embroidery, to apply them to the fabric, outlining them to hide the cut edge (some being put over the seams). But although still done commercially, the present-day designer would not choose this method for preference.

III

When there is a powdering of small units, it is possible to put soft backing into a table clamp tambour frame, then, keeping the grain of the fabrics corresponding, to put the material over this, pinning and tacking

and embroidering one or more motifs at a time.

Having completed the embroidery press over the back, stick the ends, remove from the frame and, for a chasuble, cut the backing away close up to the embroidery. When braids have been used as decoration these are stitched on to the chasuble pieces when laid out flatly; then when the final joining has been done, the last side of the braid which covers the join is slip-stitched.

An embroidered medallion, having been worked separately, would be cut out and pasted on the back. The edges may be turned over, or cut closely and later finished with a cord. It is fixed to the chasuble, its pins put in vertically, then with tiny stitches on the right side, and longer ones on the reverse, it is attached at intervals all over, and finally stitched round the outside. This may either be done with the work framed-up or spread out flatly on a table.

Methods of Transferring the Design

Choose the method best suited to the individual embroidery. When a lively drawing is reduced by neatening it up to a mechanical precision during the process of transferring, then the craftswoman has failed to choose the best method for capturing the spirit of that particular design.

Pricking and pouncing

When accuracy is required this method is still the most satisfactory. But the creative embroideress may find it a disadvantage to have a permanent line upon the fabric should an alteration be deemed an improvement; or it may be decided to develop parts of the design as the work proceeds. Alternatively, a hard line is unwanted when transparent materials are applied. These objections can, to some extent, be overcome by pricking and painting in the important lines, and marking with dots at intervals the tentative ones; or they may be tacked in before the pounce is removed.

1 Trace the design, leaving a good margin of tracing paper round the edge. It is important to think about the construction at every stage during transferring, as it is so easy to lose the drawing.

2 Mark the centres down and across, but do not prick.

3 Mark the corners or the pattern line, but only make spaced perforations. Never paint in, but mark with pins or tack before removing the pounce. This is most important because the material may stretch or contract during the process of embroidery, and the pattern must be marked again when making-up.

4 Put the tracing over a folded piece of felt, covered with tissue paper (this makes it easier to see the lines). Set a No. 9 or 10 needle in a pin vice (*129*) or make for it a little holder by folding paper, and prick all the lines with small holes, close together. Hold the tracing up to the light to see if any have been missed (*129*).

130 Pouncing

Some workers prefer to prick the front and others the back of the tracing.

Pouncing and painting

1 When practicable transfer the design, after framing-up, with the frame flatly on a table, build it up under the material with books so that the surface is firm.

2 Put the pricked tracing upon the material, checking that the centre lines on both correspond. Keep it in position with weights.

3 Black pounce consists of powdered charcoal, white, powered cuttlefish (now difficult to procure); to each a little magnesia may be added to give weight. For grey, mix the two together.

4 Dip the end of the pouncer (*130*), into the pounce; shake off surplus. Using a small circular movement rub it through the perforations. Do not go over the same section more than once and avoid replenishing with too much pounce.

5 Lift away the tracing carefully (and clean it).

6 Using a fine water-colour brush, sable No. 1 or 2, according to size of work, and water-colour, usually black, white or grey; blue upon white (a little gum arabic can be added for permanence); paint with a very fine line over the lines composed of dots of pounce; start at the part

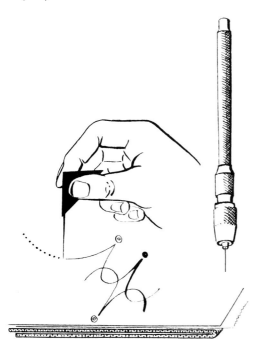

129 Transferring the design

of the design nearest to the worker and cover with a piece of paper as it proceeds. (For wool use oil-colour and turpentine.) It is important that this painting is done thoughtfully so that lines 'run through' and the drawing accurate. It is fatal if the frame is jolted during the process!

Alternatively, for less important work, it is much quicker and the line is finer if a pentol or similar pen with waterproof ink is used. (But it can spread if in contact with dampness.)

For those who prefer to draw spontaneously directly upon the fabric, pens such as the Pikaby are useful as the line can be removed with water.

7 When completed, flick away surplus pounce with a clean duster.

Alternatively, for work in the hand, or too large to frame-up in one piece, pin out the material very accurately so that it is taut, proceed as before.

Other methods

1 Keeping the perforated tracing in position with weights, dampen a pad with petrol or benzene, rub on to a cobblers' heel ball, then with a circular movement rub over all the lines.

2 Spray the fabric with methylated spirit, petrol or benzene, rub French chalk or pounce powder through the perforated tracing, then remove carefully and spray again. These are methods used commercially, as are the various perforating appliances which can be plugged in.

3 The creative embroideress may prefer to cut out the design pieces in paper, either arranging them directly upon the fabric or upon paper, tacking round the shapes or drawing around them. This is especially suitable for very large hangings. The paper forms can be exchanged for the materials cut to shape and ready to be applied.

4 Trace out the design on to tissue paper (tracing paper is too stiff and cellophane does not tear), tack through, following the lines, then tear away. This gives scope for a very free development of the design.

5 Experienced designers mark out guiding lines with tailors' chalk, or paint directly upon the fabric, creating the design in terms of fabric, and cutting out and applying materials to the background spontaneously. Sometimes they are attached with a suitable rubber solution, but this is not practical unless there is to be a covering of stitching.

FABRICS

Although the choice of fabrics suitable for vestments and hangings has not greatly changed, brocades and damasks are now recognised as making unsuitable backgrounds for embroidery, as their designs are complete in themselves.

The hand-woven 150 cm wide silk, or silk and cotton mixtures are perfect for the purpose, and are made in the liturgical colours.

Less costly and obtainable in a wide range of exciting colours are Sekers fabrics, but some will be found to be unsuitable for vestments because they crease in wear.

There are other somewhat similar furnishing fabrics.

Sanderson materials are woven in a variety of textures, some are specially good for altar frontals.

Fine wool dress materials and suitings are suitable as backgrounds, and are wide.

Then there are the Thai silks in wonderful colours, some heavier than others. They are costly and a wide range is now difficult to locate.

Indian and Chinese silks, lighter in weight, are also woven in beautiful colours, they are now more easily obtainable.

Figure 129 shows a few examples of typical materials, together with some sources of supply. (Given at the end of the book.)

Most of the synthetic lining materials are not recommended as the colours sometimes change, silks, such as Shantung are the right weight for the purpose. On the whole the natural fabrics are more predictable and are preferable to synthetic man-made fibres such as rayon which are tawdry and pretentious.

METAL THREADS

Some useful threads are shown in *figure 131*.

Nos 1–4	Japanese gold substitute – 1K, 2K, 3K, 4K. Silver 2s, 3s, 4s. Sold by the reel
5–8	Twists gold or silver No. 1, No. 1½, No. 2, No. 3, by the metre
9–11	Check gold or silver 8 × 2. 16 × 3. 36 × 6, by the metre
12–13	O.O.E. Twist 121, 122, by the skein
14	Madeira thread. Gold or silver, by the packet
15	Mex Astrella. Gold or silver, by the skein
16–19	Imitation Jap T72, T71, T70, T69, by the reel or 6 metre lengths
20	Lurex 95, by 6 metre lengths
21	Lurex gold cord, by the metre
22	Lurex 105A, by 6 metre lengths
23–28	T70 twist. 2 × 2, 3 × 2, 4 × 2, 2 × 2 × 2, 3 × 2 × 2, 4 × 2 × 2, by the metre
29	X super pearl purl, by the dram
30	Pearl purl No. 1, by the dram
31	Pearl purl No. 2, by the dram
32	Pearl purl No. 3, by the dram
33	Smooth No. 8, by the dram
34	Rough No. 8, by the dram
35	Bright check No. 8, by the dram
36	Bright check No. 5, by the dram
37	Bright check No. 1, by the dram
38	Flat bright bullion, by the dram
39	Plate, by the dram
40	Tambour, by the metre
41	Passing 6s, by the metre
42	Passing 4s, by the metre
43	Fine cord, by the metre
44	Heavy cord, by the metre
45	Russia braid, by the metre
46	Gold crepe, by the metre
47	Gold Medium Grecian, by the metre
48	Lurex cord, Gold No. 5, by the metre
49	Lurex cord, Gold No. 6, by the metre
50	Lurex cord, Gold No. 7, by the metre
51	Madeira threads. Spiral. Packets. Gold or Silver
52	No. 15. Gold or silver, by the reel
53	Lurex passing. No. 13. Gold, by the reel
54	Lurex passing. No. 13. Silver, by the reel
55	Lurex passing. No. 13. Copper, by the reel
56–57	Note case cord, by the metre Kid. Gold or silver, by the 2.5 cm square
58	Flat gold, by the reel
59	Light gold twist, by the reel
60	Black twisted with gold, by the reel
61	Thicker black cord (16 ply) twisted with gold, by the reel
29–47	Admiralty quality will tarnish less.

For church-embroidery today all types of thread are used: they are selected for qualities of texture or for the type of line which can be produced. For example, chenille might be contrasted with a metal thread. Apart from aesthetic considerations, the choice will be determined by suitability for the purpose and in relation to the scale of the design and the fabrics; and also durability.

Maltese silk (or *couching* or *horsetail*) is a

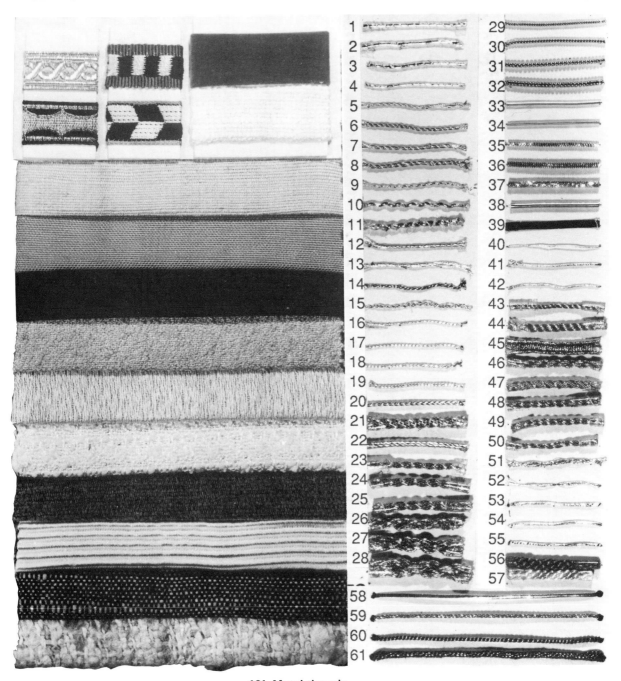

131 Metal threads
See stockists page 173

tightly twisted, strong silk used for *couching down* gold or silver; it should be waxed and is also used for sewing down cords and synthetic braids.

Fine *silk cords*, some twisted with a metal thread, also very fine coloured silk cords and the conventional round cords; these are sewn through and not over.

Most of the *braids and trimmings* are intended to be completely decorative in themselves, therefore the few examples shown in *figure 131* are typical of those which can form the basis for further development in terms of embroidery.

The sew-on, unmounted jewels would probably be most useful to the present-day designer.

The fabrics shown in *figure 131* are typical of the type of texture and weave most likely to be of interest to those working in the idiom of the day.

The development of braids woven with synthetic metallic threads opens up immense possibilities, as they are untarnishable and inexpensive; but many are over-bright and glittering. An additional danger is that not all will withstand hard wear, and will crack and then break at folds or where perforated by stitches. Therefore these braids should be selected with foresight, bearing in mind that some are exactly what are needed for expressing contemporary design, and others can do nothing but cheapen and degrade.

The selected examples shown in *figure 131* have been found to be satisfactory for church embroidery; it is advisable to use a fairly fine strong thread, waxed, and a fine needle, to sew into, and not over, the tubular and flat braids.

The directions for manipulating these threads and braids are given in the section dealing with goldwork.

'Lurex' covered thread, size 13, in gold, copper or silver introduces the alternative metallic colour; it is a round thread, made on the principle of a passing thread, but is not intended to be used threaded into the needle. It should be *couched down*, either double or single; it is pliant, and very satisfactory, provided that the couching stitches are kept a little closer together than usual.

Plate is a narrow, flat continuous strip of gold, it possesses a characteristic gleam, which gives a richness which is unique. It is advisable to buy the Admiralty quality, as it is much less likely to tarnish. To start and end, fold back a little hook, stitch through this.

Passing thread and *tambour threads* can be threaded into the needle for stitching or couched down double or single. As aluminium does not tarnish it is recommended as a substitute for silver which discolours quickly. The methods for working are shown in the goldwork section.

For Russia and other flat braids, it is advisable either to sew into them with slanting stitches or to attach with back stitches or running stitches along the centre vein. They bend easily.

The wire threads, purls and bullions, etc, used for ceremonial embroideries and for heraldic badges and masonic regalia are outside the scope of the present work, but the techniques are fully dealt with in other titles (see further reading page 172). But as plate, passing and tambour threads belong to this group, a short explanation relating to the qualities is necessary.

The best quality, that which includes the greatest proportion of pure gold (or silver), is known as Admiralty or Government standard and is always recommended as being less likely to tarnish.

The second quality is known as *gold*, and that with the least pure metal in it is *gilt*, which, in common with tinsel, will tarnish.

Professional workers purchase these goods by weight, but as the amateur only needs comparatively small quantities, these are supplied by the metre by firms listed at the end of the book.

Metal Thread Embroidery

Gold was synonymous with religious embroidery, but even before the discontinuance of the making of Japanese gold and silver, greater emphasis was placed upon design which made a definite statement in colour and weave. With the increasing use of machine embroidery, gold has become less important because that thread is fine and lacks the richness associated with traditional goldwork.

Characteristic of church embroidery is still, however, the inclusion of metal threads; this calls for a proper understanding of the nature and possibilities of the technique so that it may better serve the creative designer. The traditional methods possess a unique quality, but the application needs to be re-examined in relation to the contemporary idiom. Also the rigidity of conventional church work technique is too limiting and constricting for the seemingly spontaneous and vigorous approach to present-day design; yet the play of light, the richness and the textures can be apreciated as too valuable to discard, and new ways of adopting the goldwork methods have to be thought out.

In this type of embroidery several factors are inter-dependent and these require special knowledge, skill and experience; for example, the satisfactory interpretation of a design depends not only upon the symbolic meaning, but the choice of method, and the construction, whether or not it conforms to the requirements imposed by its purpose when used.

With the emphasis concentrated upon the need for more lively design, it is important that certain technical considerations should not be neglected. First, vestments, etc, are subjected to hard wear and a long life, therefore durability must to some extent govern the choice of materials, threads and stitchery. This applies especially to the couching thread as this wears out before the metal thread. With the desire to retain the freedom of line it is a temptation to put the stitches too far apart. Secondly, because of their attractive appearance sometimes unsuitable synthetic cords and braids are used; the variety covered with foil will split where it is bent or stitched, and will not wear for more than a short time. Thirdly, the stitch treatment should be suited to the purpose for which it is intended. For instance, a basket-filling over string is stiff and heavy and would prevent a chasuble or draped frontal from falling in graceful folds. Fourthly, the threads and size of stitching should be in scale with the material and design.

This type of embroidery must be worked in a frame, so that both hands are free for manipulating the threads, and, the material being kept taut, the tension of the stitching is correct and puckering is avoided. A certain amount of practice is necessary before a rhythm of movement is attained.

The substitute for Japanese gold and silver threads are made in 4 sizes, the thickest being almost equivalent to K2. It is pliant and pleasant to use, but 'brassy' in appearance. This thread, also passing and tambour are laid on the surface of the material, and couched down (*132A*). For this can be used Maltese silk (very fine), stranded cotton or sewing silk (neither is really strong enough to withstand wear) or Gütermann Polyester 100 m spools, colour 893. Whichever thread is used it is generally passed through bees-wax for additional strength and ease in working.

Metal threads, including Japanese gold (when obtainable) are couched down, usually two, side by side. Some thick synthetic or real threads can be sewn down singly. If colour is required embroidery or sewing silk can be used.

Figure 132A Start by bending one thread back to the length required, forming a loop, and take a stitch into this. The subsequent couching stitches are taken over the metal threads at regular intervals; they must be sufficiently wide to avoid nipping the gold into a waist.

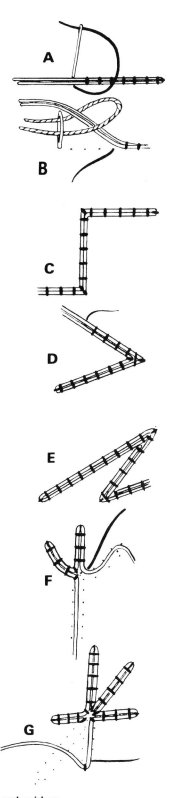

132 Gold embroidery

Figure 132B At the end of a row cut the metal threads, leaving about 2 cm. Take about 25 cm of fairly thick silk, bend it double and thread the loop into a chenille needle. Then thread the ends of the gold into this loop (or they can be threaded directly into the eye of the needle). The needle then pulls the ends through to the back where they will be pasted back later. With experience it will be found expedient to leave the ends upon the surface for as long as possible, because when once they have been taken through, the orange silk 'core' is apt to become entangled with subsequent stitching and brought up to the front again. It used to be the practice to do the goldwork after completing the other stitching.

Figure 132C To keep the spaces between the couching stitches regular, it is necessary to treat the turn at the corner in one of two ways according to the position of the previous stitch.

Figure 132D When a point is not too sharp the threads can be turned.

Figure 132E For a very sharp point only the outer thread is bent round (a stiletto is of assistance when manipulating the turn), the inside being taken up to the point and cut (leaving 1.5 cm). A new thread is inserted farther away from the point, and the couching is continued. Always exaggerate the sharpness of a point by taking the turn slightly beyond the traced line.

Figure 132F With forethought, unnecessary ends can be avoided by turning a single thread, stitching it and couching the two together on the return.

Figure 133A When there are two or more rows of metal threads, the couching stitches are bricked. To build up a narrow block, a single thread may be taken from side to side, the couching thread is passed underneath to be brought out on the opposite side so as to be in position for sewing down the doubled thread on the return.

Figure 133B The most useful method for turning the gold or other metal thread is shown. It will be seen that one new thread is introduced at each turn.

Figure 133C For large blocks, where double metal threads can be turned at the end of each row, alternative methods for stitching are given. It is no longer con-

sidered essential to cover the edges with a cord or couching; an outline is only used where the design needs emphasis.

Many points common to all gold couching are illustrated in diagram (*135*) bearing in mind that the most straightforward method is usually the best.

133 Couching metal threads

134 Cockerel worked in couched metal threads

135 Stole designed by Sylvia Green, worked by Pam Waterworth

Padding with felt

For an intricate shape, put the perforated tracing upon the felt, and pounce, and if necessary paint on the design.

Figure 136A Cut the first padding fairly small, secure by sticking or stitching at the top, bottom and sides, then complete the stitching. (This only applies for larger shapes.) It is sometimes possible to stick round the edges of the felt to keep it in place, using an adhesive such as *Copydex*.

Figure 136B Cut the second layer a little larger, secure in the same way.

Figure 136C The third and final padding is cut to the outline and stitched just within the line. It is obvious that complicated three-dimensional modelling can be carried out in this way. The felt should be as nearly as possible the same colour as the metal thread. For larger objects one layer of felt may be put over the whole shape before couching.

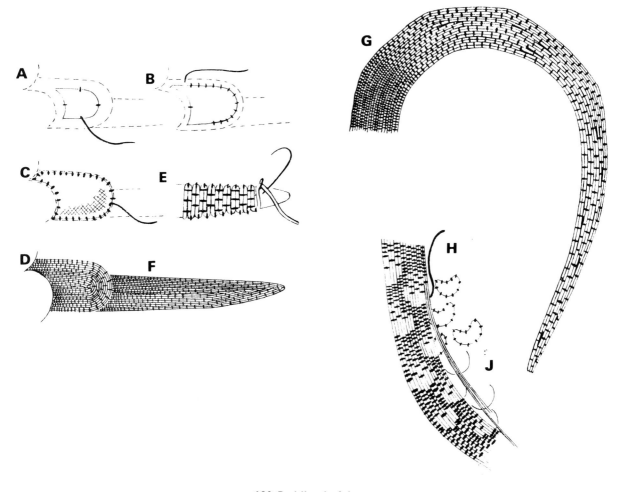

136 Padding in felt

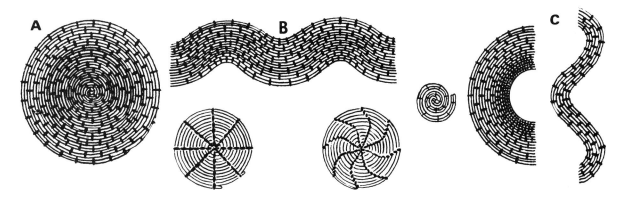

137 Using metal threads

Figure 136D In the small wing feather, the metal threads are taken round the outline and stitched right through the padding. Colour and spacing can enhance the effect. The cut ends would probably have to be taken through one at a time.

Figure 136E For the longer narrow wing feathers and similar shapes, a single, fine thread might be taken backwards and forwards across the width. A stiletto helps in the manipulating of the turns. Alternatively such a shape might be worked as shown in the next diagram (*F*).

Figure 136F Here the outside threads follow the outline, and the inner ones terminate to form a vein, and are taken through singly. This requires skill and practice as the core of the thread may be exposed.

Figure 136G The play of light will determine the direction and placing of the metal threads. It takes experience to decide when to let the gold threads disappear, singly, by taking them through to the back.

To work the tail feathers and similar tapering shapes so that the shine is unbroken, it is advisable to start each double row at the wider end, retaining a few threads to run right through; for this the outside, the centre, and one or two more would be selected. The remainder of the threads are gradually 'lost' by being taken through to the back, as shown in the diagram. This requires careful forethought in order that the remaining threads may be reformed into pairs and the couching stitches bricked. An alternative arrangement would be to start with two threads right down the centre; then on either side the threads would terminate at the outline as would each subsequent row; each thread of which would have to be taken down separately at the edge.

Figure 136H This treatment of the breast feathers is a variation of the previous method (*G*) with the shapes cut in parchment or card.

Figure 136J The Italian method of couching gold (without padding) could be used for the lower feathers.

Figure 137A One of the most effective uses for metal threads is for the spiral filling of a circle. Here it is started on the perimeter and the stitches are widely spread; they are then bricked until they become crowded, then the spacing is changed to anticipate leaving out about one in every four stitches. With each subsequent row fewer stitches are retained. By planning ahead the spacing is kept as even as possible, as no two stitches should be directly under each other.

Figure 137B The play of light upon a wavy border embroidered with metal

threads is most rewarding. But here the centre row is worked first with regularly spaced couching stitches; the modifications on either side can be followed from the diagram.

Figure 137C The semicircle is planned to be stitched in colour, and this becomes more dense towards the centre.

Invariably it is preferable to work out the most straightforward plan for the direction of the rows of metal threads which are to fill a given shape. By starting double rows at the centre top and bottom of the arms of a cross it ensures that the middle will be satisfactorily filled (*138A*). An alternative way of treating the surrounding area is by taking the rows all the way round, turning the corners so that there is a diagonal line of stitches. This is decorative as it accentuates the change in the direction of the gold.

Figure 138B shows a further example of the treatment of another type of shape; here either single or double metal threads are stitched over with a contrasting colour in diagonal lines. There are endless variants which can be produced by spacing the stitches to form different patterns. Because of the complexity of the shape, the rows are taken straight downwards and each end would be taken through to the back.

Figure 139, shows the type of design which, if carried out with contrasting thicknesses of gold, in rhythmical rows, will catch the light to advantage. A fine couching thread should be used. Invisible super soft nylon thread is useful for such work, but it may lead to the fabric puckering.

Figure 140 shows another example which shows how repetition and the play of light on the couched metal threads could be used to advantage.

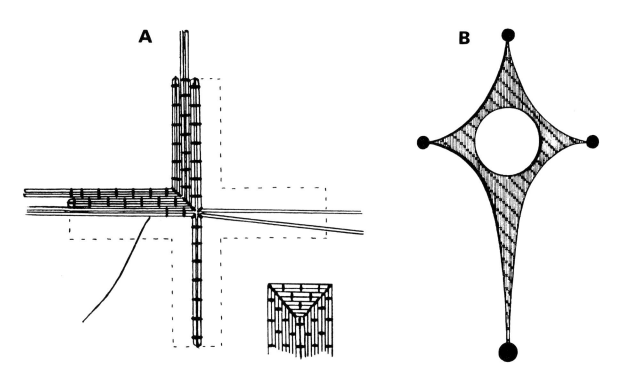

138 Manipulating Jap Gold substitute

139 Designing for metal thread work

140 Play of light on couched metal threads

Figure 141A The Tree of Life. Use singly, a flexible thread, such as Lurex covered passing No. 13. At wider intervals than usual, stitch over with a dark thread.

Figure 141B Although a two- or three-ply twist is effective, almost any metal thread can be used either singly or double. For the colour sewing any silk thread will wear better than a mercerised one. If the pattern to be stitched covers the ground evenly, the background may not require stitching down, except at the edges; self-colour thread is used when this is necessary.

Figure 141C For the foundation of Burden Stitch passing or tambour is threaded into the needle and long 'laid' stitches are spaced in horizontal rows. Then stitches are worked over these in one or more colours so that the metal glints through. Large areas can be carried out in this method. Where required, lines can be

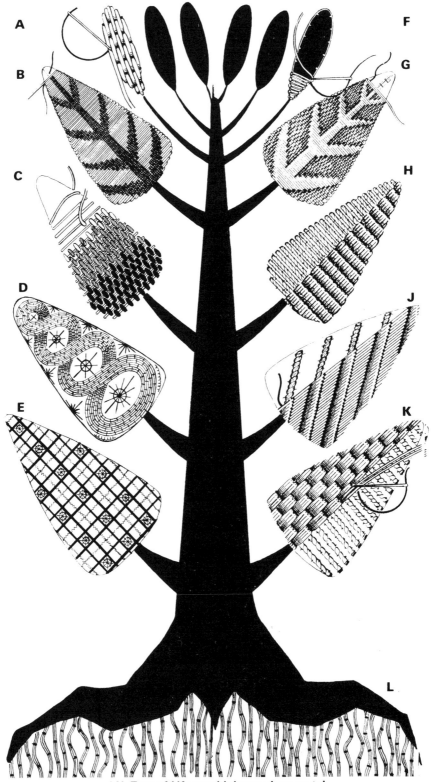

141 Tree of Life combining various metal threads

defined by superimposed stitchery (ie split stitch) or cord.

Figure 141D The effect of interlacing may be accentuated by stitch-spacing and colour changes. One method is to start by working a part of the pattern which is underneath, then work the thread which go over these, stopping before they again become the upper ones, put them aside, and place the first group in position over the second, stitch them down, until they in turn become the under-group, and the first group can be put over again.

By using several groups of metal threads of different types of colour, interesting effects can be obtained.

The alternative method is to cut off the ends of the metal threads and take them through to the back, starting again on the other side of the junction of the interlaced lines. This effect is flatter than it is when the groups of threads are actually stitched one over the other.

Figure 141E A great variety of tartan filling patterns can be devised by stitching down at spaced intervals metal threads of differing textures and widths.

Interesting open fillings can be invented.

Figure 141F This method is only suitable for narrower forms. From parchment, thin leather or card, cut out the shape a fraction smaller. Selecting a suitable thickness of tambour, passing or plate, bend it backwards and forwards across the template, stitching the turns with a fine waxed thread which is passed underneath and brought up on the opposite side in place for the next stitch.

Figure 141G This effect can be obtained in several ways. The illustration shows that the veins of the leaf have been padded with a bunch of linen raising thread cut into the required lengths and sewn down with cotton; but laid or split stitches might have been worked with the raising thread itself. The metal thread has been taken right across and the background stitched with a darker thread.

The padding might have been done with

string or felt.

Almost the same effect could have been achieved by the Italian method of couching gold; for, although no padding is used, the pattern appears to be raised. For this double metal threads are taken either down or across the shape. The background is couched, the bricking being spaced at regular intervals, but it is not fastened down where it passes over the pattern.

Figure 141H For all the variations of basketwork string is sewn down in evenly spaced rows, leaving at least the width of the string between each row. Using metal threads or stout floss it is taken over two rows of string and stitched down with waxed thread, which may be secured with a tiny back stitch into the fabric, as this leaves the hands free to manipulate the gold.

Figure 141J First stitch down the lines of string. It is probably more satisfactory to sew over the metal threads singly for these diagonal lines.

Figure 141K There are many other basket stitch patterns, but this arrangement is good for small areas.

Figure 141L Waved gold, useful for an irregular texture; the rows could be closer together.

Metal threads and braids can be combined with various media, such as spray dyeing. The examples given are restricted to basic methods. At *A* in *figure 142* the small leaves would be thin leather, skived or kid, sewn with tiny stitches or attached with a fabric adhesive. Too often the shapes are too small and isolated, the whole effect is thin, this applies to *142B* also, but by using several cords and braids together the width can be increased. At *142C* the effect of this technique is shown (it is not a working drawing). The raised shapes are cut in felt stuck down, a double row of metal threads is taken across, and these are stitched over with darker stranded cotton, for the following row the stitches are bricked over another pair of metal threads. The raised areas should not be too wide.

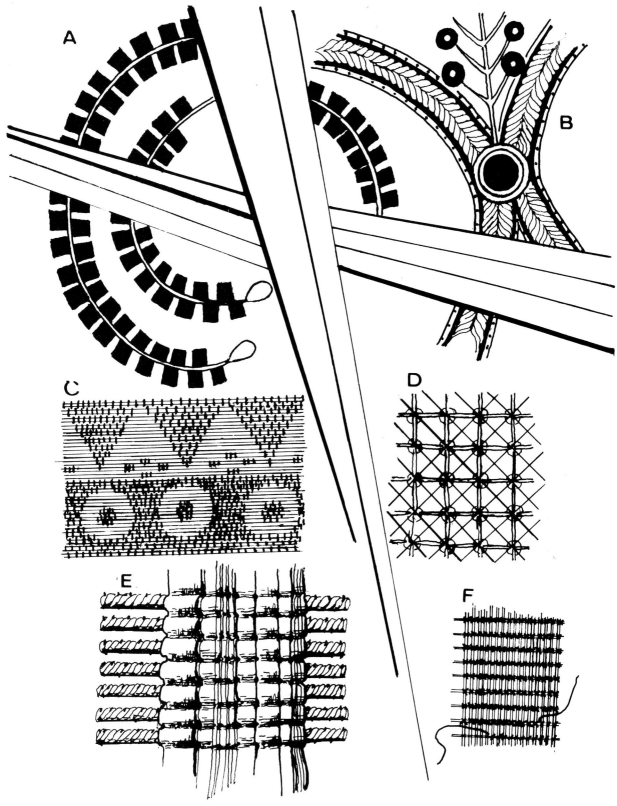

142 Metal Thread techniques

Figure 142D shows a fairly open filling. Two thicknesses of metal thread would be used, because it can be threaded into the needle. The fine threads are taken across and down, these are crossed diagonally with the thicker one. A fine needle and thread is taken up through the sequin at the intersections, the stitch goes over and is taken down through the hole in the sequin. *Basket stitch* is the basis for *142E*. The foundation of string is sewn down, over these leather thongs, plate, silk or narrow ribbon, which is sewn down between the rows of string. Another filling is shown at *142F*, again passing thread would be used, downwards and across. These are stitched with a little cross at the intersections.

143 A Basket stitch filling, varying the thickness of gold threads

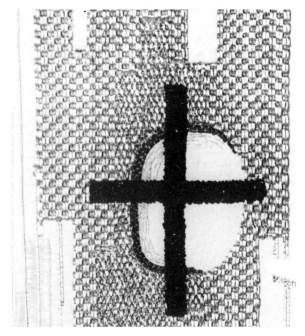

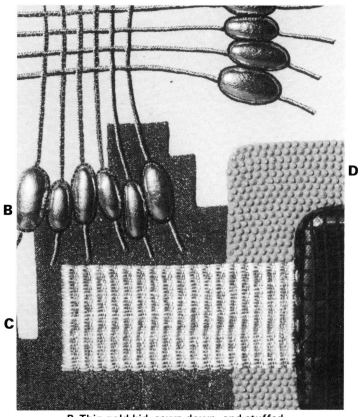

B Thin gold kid, sewn down, and stuffed with wool
C A narrow silver tubular braid, flattened, and sewn over rows of string
D Flat beads attached with a small matching bead

Sewing Down Cords, etc

To preserve the spontaneity of a design, the technical methods must be selected with understanding. The linear character of the sketch (*145*) calls for various cords, etc; some suitable methods are given in diagrammatic form (*146*). Many of the finer lines could be stitched on an embroidery machine.

To sew plate

Start by bending the end of the plate to form a little hook, then with a waxed thread (Maltese silk or cotton), take a stitch through it (*146A*). For a crinkled line first hold the plate along the length of a screw or a comb and indent it with the thumb nail; it is then sewn across (*146A,B*). Where a straight flat line is required, the sewing-down stitches are taken across at regular spacing. Before reaching the end make another little hook and stitch it down. Where a wider line is to be worked, first stitch down a padding of felt, string or cord, if this is thought necessary. Then fold the plate backwards and forwards, taking a stitch into each bend (*146C*). Many other threads can be worked in this way. For the flat 'Lurex' or a passing thread, etc, the spacing can be altered (*146D*).

When a very fine tambour thread is used for stitching (*146E*) it may be threaded directly into the needle, but for other tam-

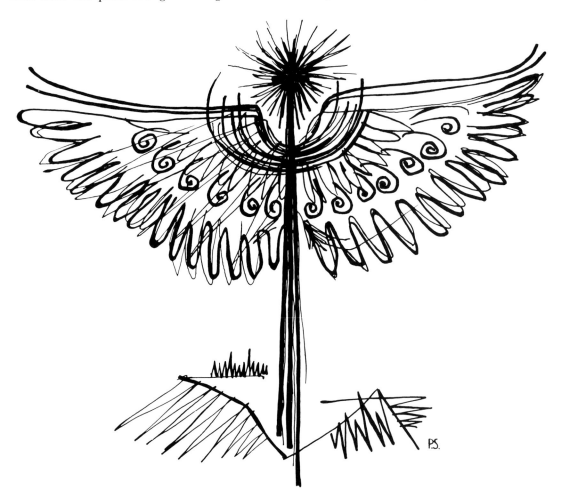

144 Linear character of sketch which calls for various cords

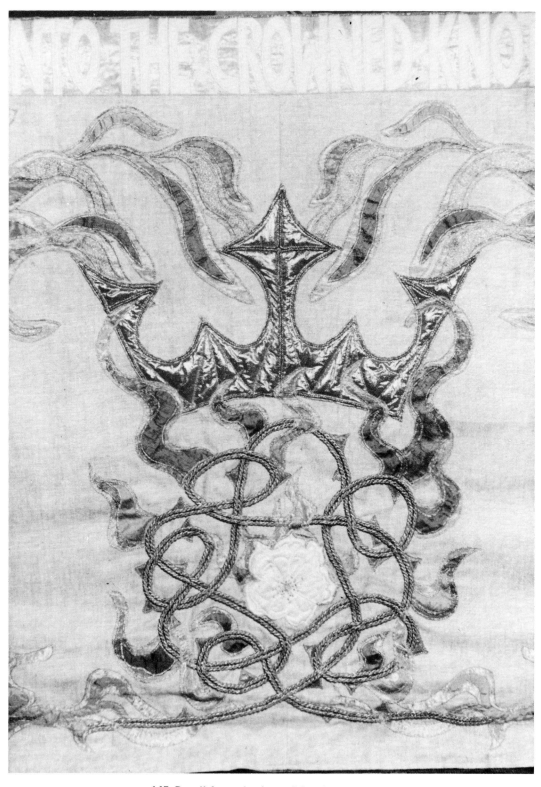

145 Detail from the frontal for the nave altar,
Westminster Abbey, by Belinda Scarlett. See
also figure 100

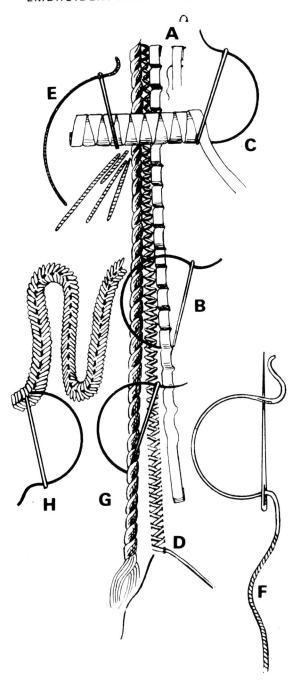

146 Methods for sewing down cords

bour and passing threads, untwist the metal thread, leaving about 5 cm of the silk core exposed. Then thread this into the needle, put the point through it close to the end and, holding it between the thumb and first finger, pull it through (*146F*). This will not come unthreaded while working, and prevents the metal thread from tearing the fabric. Many stitches can be worked with these threads.

To sew twisted cords
Using a waxed sewing thread (Maltese silk or Gütermann 100% Polyester), take the stitch at the same slant as the twist of the cord (*146G*). The needle goes down through the cord between the twists, and not right across it. The stitches can be made alternately on one side of the cord then on the other; this is essential when turning a corner, or a point. Here, it helps if the cord is first pinched into a point and, after stitching the point is again pressed into shape with a stiletto.

To begin and end a cord or any narrow braid, leave an end of about 1.5 cm, pierce a hole with a stiletto and either thread the end into a chenille needle or thread it into a 'sling' and pull it through to the back (*132B*), where it can be unravelled and then pressed out flatly and stuck down.

To sew Russia and similar braids
These can be back-stitched or stab-stitched along the centre (*146H*), or they can be stitched alternately on either side, with stitches which slant with the threads of braid. (In a true Russia braid, the inside threads can be pulled up; the braid will then form curves easily.) For a narrow flat braid it is sometimes effective to bend it over at points and corners, when it can be sewn down with small stitches taken invisibly into the edges (*147A*).

Most of the flat and tubular or rat-tail braids can be bent and turned freehand. A pin will keep it in place until stitched. The fine circular threads will bend and can be sewn with a fine thread (*147B*).

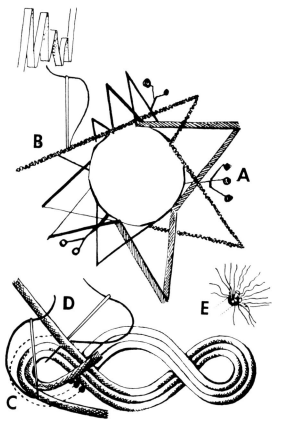

147 Sewing on Russia and similar braids

The thicker, filled circular braids ('Lurex' covered), can either be sewn with a small stitch into each side alternately (*147C*) or the needle can be passed right through the braid from side to side. Then the needle will penetrate the material to be brought up in position for the next stitch (*147D*). It is advisable to use a fine needle as this damages these synthetic threads less, and the sewing thread should be waxed.

Invariably it is satisfactory to start and finish by allowing an extra 2 cm of the braid, then pierce holes with the stiletto, and take them through to the wrong side with a chenille needle, with or without a 'sling'. On the back the ends can be cut down to 1.5 cm and frayed out, then pasted down. But where there is a filling, the result may be flatter, if, after fraying out, the core is cut away (*147E*) before stitching the ends down.

EMBROIDERY TECHNIQUES

Some techniques are more suited to interpreting the designs for church usage than are others. The following are suggestions which may be helpful.

Laidwork

Use a frame for laidwork, and only slightly twisted threads. This is a useful method for interpreting flat washes of colour such as intended for the centre of the formalised pomegranate (*149A*). According to the shape, decide whether the direction of the stitches should be vertical or horizontal. It will be seen from the diagram (*149B*) that the thread is taken across the surface; the needle only penetrates at the edges, being brought up exactly beside the point where it was put in. These long stitches can be caught down unobtrusively by crossing them with a divided or fine self-coloured

157

thread; these stitches, spaced at regular intervals, have to be kept in place with tiny stitches, which are bricked (*149C*). But a decorative treatment might be preferred for the pomegranate such as illustrated in *figure D, E, F and G*. Important to the carrying out of a modern design is the couched line (*149H*). This consists of a group of threads (the number and thickness of the threads can be varied) laid along the line, and stitched across at right angles with a finer thread. Half the final number of threads may be bent over to form a loop for the commencement. And at the end of the line, they are cut off at about 2 cm and taken through with a 'sling' as for gold. *Figure 150A* illustrates broken effects obtainable with laidwork, contrasted with hard outlines, which might be couched or worked in split stitch. This is worked from right to left, the needle being brought up in the middle of each previous stitch (*150C*) and put down ahead.

By working several rows of split stitches, a solid filling can be built up, which, on a curve, catches the light. Many stitches are suitable for tying down the laidwork in a decorative way.

Innumerable openlaid fillings can be invented and some which are worked over a foundation of crossed threads, tied down at the inter-sections, are shown in *figure 150B*.

Patchwork

Patchwork has become popular both for secular and religious purposes, the traditional methods have been adapted and developed. Absolute accuracy is still essential.

Not only are the shapes of the patches made in varying sizes, but fabrics of entirely different weights and textures are used. Therefore the thickness of the template is adjusted to compensate where necessary, as they remain in place, if this is considered to

148 St Peter, carried out entirely in laidwork, by Beryl Dean, 1954. This work is now in the Victoria and Albert Museum collection

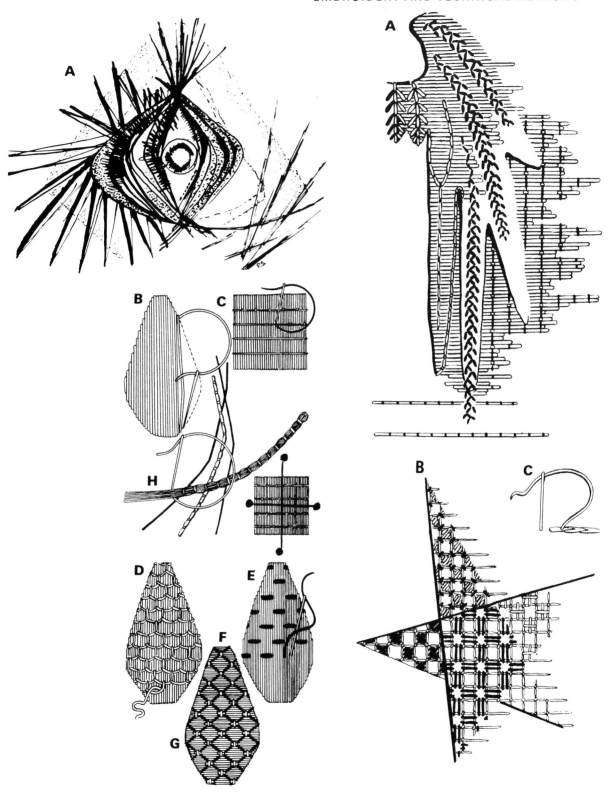

149 Laidwork

150 Laidwork

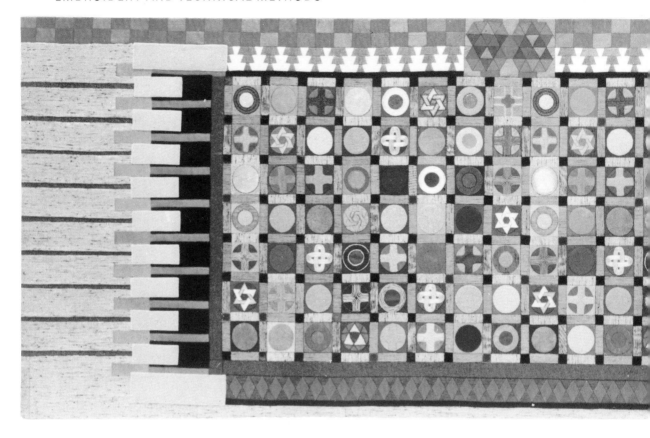

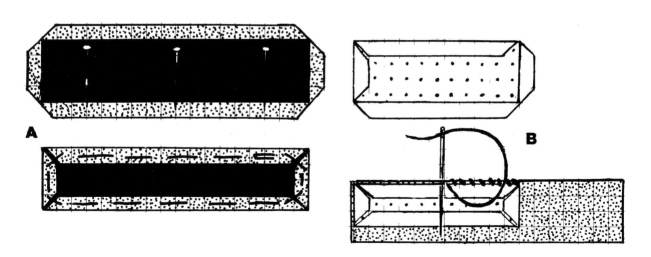

152 Patchwork method

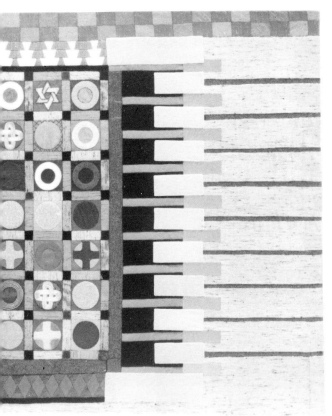

151 Frontal for the Chapel of the Westminster Hospital by Beryl Dean 1969. Patchwork in various materials including metallic gauzes

and tacked, starting with a backstitch (instead of a knot) as this facilitates the withdrawing of the tacks. However, with practise, and very great care the turnings can be stuck down (it is risky as the front of the work may be marked), but it is essential that an absolute minimum should be used. Copydex is a suitable adhesive.

The next stage (152B) is to put the right sides of two templates together and to overcast each edge, joining on adjoining patches, completing a section at a time. Then joining these up, as continuous lines can be kept straight.

Appliqué

This is one of the most widely used methods, as the broad effects which the application of the material makes possible are especially suited to the church's needs. For large and small curtains, hangings, banners, frontals and palls, etc, appliqué combined with hand and machine embroidery will give the effect for which the creative embroideress is striving.

Fabrics are selected for their colour and for their textural qualities; transparent materials and nets are important; so, too, are pieces with printed or woven patterns.

When intended for church use, appliqué has to withstand really hard wear, therefore careful preparation is advisable. This will also help to overcome the possibility of puckering.

be an advantage. By deliberately exploiting contrasting directions in the weave of the material, the play of light becomes important.

It was Avril Colby who in 1954 introduced patchwork into use for the church with the cope and mitre for Burford.

Less technically conventional is the altar frontal (151). For its construction the templates were cut in *Vilene*, the choice of weight chosen to compensate when thin fabrics were used. For the centre squares thin Lurex tissue covered with net, and embroidered, were mounted over a heavy *Vilene*. The templates of the smallest squares had to be considerably reduced in size, because of the thickness of the millinery velvet with which they were covered.

Traditionally, the material was cut with a turning (152A) which was folded over

1 Whether the background is mounted in a frame or not, trace or tack out the main lines of the design.

2 Mark out and cut the pieces to be applied so that the grain of the material corresponds with that of the background. Allow extra on edges which are underneath (153A). Top left wing.

If the work is to be carried out in blind appliqué (which is stronger) allow turnings on all edges, those on the outside are turned under as shown in (153).

3 Starting with the pieces which are underneath, and finishing with those on

153(a) The preparation of appliqué for the edges of convex and concave curves

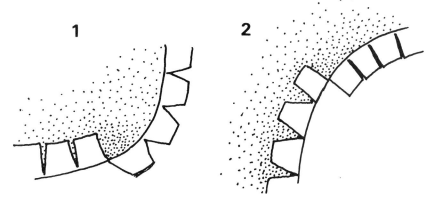

153(b) Detail of convex and concave curves in blind appliqué

top, pin in place, keeping the pins horizontal. With small stitches attach to the
background along the design lines
(*153A*). Secure with vertical lines of zigzag tacking (*153B*). (If a frame is used,
this is done when it is a little slack; on
completion, tighten it up. Alternatively,
this preparation is done whilst the
material is laid out flatly on a table.)

4 Hem down cut edges, but where the
outlines are turned in (this can be done
either before or after the pieces are
attached), slip-stitch or invisibly hem to
the background.

5 Where the outline needs emphasising, a
strong line, such as couching or some
broad stitch, can be used. In other
places, where a broken or soft effect is
planned, stitches such as herringbone,
detached chain, seeding, etc are useful.

6 Surface decoration can be added by
stitchery, braids or machine embroidery.

A greater degree of freedom and spontaneity can be achieved by building the
whole design in cut paper shapes, which are
later substituted for similar shapes cut out
in fabric, others being rendered in stitchery.

Amateurs seldom use pasting to give
additional substance to fabrics. And it is
not advisable to use iron-on *Vilene* (or substitutes) on thin materials.

With the benefit of experience materials
can be pasted, they can then be cut without
fear of fraying and are less likely to pucker,
but this detracts from the beauty of the
fabrics as does bonding.

To mix a paste take 85 grams flour (not
self-raising) and a small teaspoonful of
resin; also 0.28 litres of cold distilled or
filtered water. Mix until smooth; strain if
necessary. Bring to the boil, stirring con-
stantly. Lessen the heat until the paste
becomes slightly transparent, allow to cool.
(A little boracic, formalin or a crystal of
thymol added to the paste will prevent
mould forming, if the church is damp.)
Frame-up a piece of muslin; apply the
paste evenly with a large brush or palette
knife. Place the material, right side up (or
several smaller pieces), on to this, and with
a clean soft cloth stroke and smooth it
outwards from the centre. Turn the frame
over and remove surplus paste with a bone
folder. Allow to dry.

Appliqué worked in a frame will only
need to be pressed over on the back with a
warm iron. If there is no metal thread a *very
slightly* and evenly damped cloth may be
used, if it will not harm the fabrics.

Only if the materials will take it, can the
whole work be stretched out (usually right
side uppermost), over a damp cloth; drawing-pins or nails being used. It is important
to keep the corners at right angles to the
sides. Allow to dry off before removing. For
further information see the section on *Canvas Work*.

Machine Embroidery

Increasingly important is machine embroidery in its own right, as an artform. Many examples will be found amongst the examples shown. There are many different types of machines, but even with a domestic model there is quite a lot of potential.

Many threads, heavy yarns and braids can be couched down, and large scale effects can be achieved by this means. But, as with hand embroidery, the basic technique for larger areas is appliqué. In *figures 154* and *155* it can be seen combined with various machine stitched methods.

Machine embroidery combines well with

154 Detail of part of an orphrey for a cope for Chester Cathedral by Judy Barry and Beryl Patten, 1981. Shows Irish, Cornely and Bernina machine embroidery

hand work, appliqué and the use of fabric dyes and transfer dye inks and spraying.

Many textures can be achieved, the experiments photographed show various methods, and hand embroidered goldwork techniques can be reproduced by machine (*156A, B* and *157A, B*).

There are several books which deal with all the developments in machine embroidery, these are recommended because the subject is vast and outside the scope of this book.

155 Detail of part of an orphrey for a cope for Chester Cathedral by Judy Barry and Beryl Patten, 1981. Shows Irish, Cornely and Bernina machine embroidery

156 A Experiments in various machine stitched surfaces for possible use in church embroidery

B Irish machine, eyelet and appliqué
methods used as a base for hand metal
thread techniques

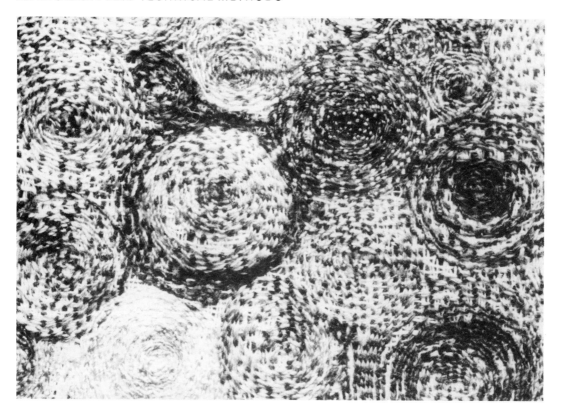

**157 Experiments in various machine-made
surfaces. Irish machine**

ETTERING

should be well spaced, balanced and pro-portioned, above all it should be legible. The pattern-value of good lettering cannot be over-emphasised, nor can the import-ance of the position of the lettering in relation to the subject matter of the design.

Although several embroidery methods are suitable appliqué is generally used for large-scale work, and this is an instance when pasting is advisable. The outlines can be defined with one or more cords (*158A*). The diagram shows that the edge has been sewn with small stitches (*158B*) and the cord attached with a fine strong thread.

For banners and other conventional pur-poses the appliqué can be carried out using bonded or other non-fraying materials such as felt or thin leather, for other materials iron-on *Vilene* (or substitutes) will prevent the edges and serifs from fraying.

A more sensitive rendering which will bring out the differences in weight and relative widths of line, can be produced by outlining the letter with split-stitch and filling in with long and short stitch and possibly adding an outline of fine cord or a doubled imitation Jap gold thread, to keep angles and points sharp each thread should be sewn separately.

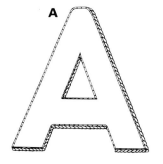

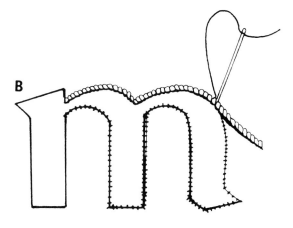

158 A–C Lettering

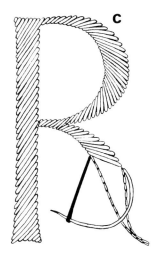

Slanting or straight satin stitch (*158C*) is the most usual method. The direction has to be carefully planned, and the slant increased to negotiate curves.

Many other embroidery techniques can be adapted for interpreting decorative lettering.

Lettering plays an increasingly important part in decoration, especially for church use.

159 Stole end embellished with machine stitching and simple hand embroidery by Pat Russell

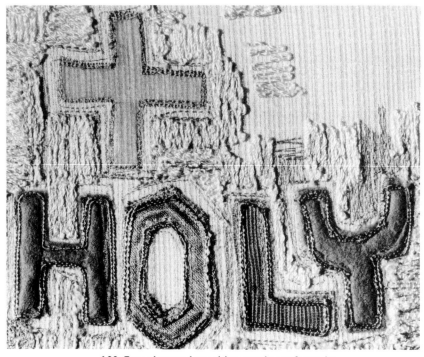

160 Experimental machine-made surfaces in conjunction with applied letter forms

EMBROIDERED HEADS

Long and short and split stitch, etc

This method can be adapted for many purposes as gradation of colours is possible. The working of long and short stitch can be followed from *figure 161A, B, C,* where the stitches are shown converging towards the centre; the number of stitches will be reduced towards the centre. When one shape overlaps another, complete the under-one first, then outline the upper shape with split stitch (*161C*) before working the long and short stitches which form the first row. These are followed by stitches all of the same length.

The conventional stitchery for heads, hands and feet, etc, is long and short stitch; the direction is straight down with changes of colour and outlining to suggest the features (*161D, E*). For narrow spaces, satin stitch is convenient. If the stitches terminate and start either side of the traced line (*161E*), these voided lines enable the features to be 'redrawn' with split stitch. Hair and beard and drapery are generally carried out in split stitch following the direction of the line. However freely the features are expressed, the basic construction or form of the head is felt in terms of embroidery.

A less rigid way of working heads, etc, is to allow the stitchery to follow the direction of the features. *Figure 161F* shows one suggestion.

161 The treatment of heads in embroidery

Interesting ways of interpreting the head are achieved by couching threads and cords by using split stitch to form spirals, and building up the features with continuous lines. This approach brings out the decorative qualities in preference to the more realistic.

Figure 162 shows how a head can be carried out in split and long and short stitch, leaving areas of the background to express the form.

162 'The Christ Child'. Detail from 'Adoration' panel by Beryl Dean for St George's Chapel, Windsor Castle

FURTHER READING

CAMPBELL-HARDING, VALERIE and WATTS, PAMELA, *Machine Embroidery: Stitch Techniques*, Batsford 1989

CHILD, HEATHER and COLLES, DOROTHY, *Christian Symbols*, Bell 1971

CHRISTIE, MRS ARCHIBALD, *Samplers and Stitches*, Batsford 1929

CLUCAS, JOY, *Your Machine for Embroidery*, Bell 1975

COLEMAN, ANNE, *The Creative Sewing Machine*, Batsford 1979

DAWSON, BARBARA, *White Work Embroidery*, Batsford 1987

DEAN, BERYL, *Ecclesiastical Embroidery*, Batsford 1958, paperback 1989

GRAY, JENNIFER, *Machine Embroidery*, Batsford 1973

GREEN, SYLVIA, *Canvas Embroidery for Beginners*, Studio Vista 1971

HOWARD, CONSTANCE, *Inspiration for Embroidery*, Batsford 1966, paperback 1985, *Embroidery and Colour*, Batsford 1976, paperback 1986, *Twentieth Century Embroidery in Great Britain*, Volume 1 to 1939 Batsford 1981, Volume 2 1940–1963 Batsford 1983, Volume 3 1964–1977 Batsford 1984, Volume 4 From 1978 Batsford 1986

LEMON, JANE, *Metal Thread Embroidery*, Batsford 1987

RUSSELL, PAT, *Lettering for Embroidery*, Batsford 1971 and 1985

WHYTE, KATHLEEN, *Design in Embroidery*, Batsford 1969, new edition 1983

SUPPLIERS OF MATERIALS AND EQUIPMENT

Mace and Nairn: Embroidery Specialists
89 Crane Street
Salisbury
Wiltshire
SP1 2PY
All embroidery materials, including linen, canvas, felt, dowlas, etc. All threads, including metal threads Nos 1 to 57 as shown in figure 131,

Stephen Simpson (Tinsel products) Limited
Avenham Road Works
PO Box 30
Preston
Lancashire
PR1 3UH
Many synthetic gold and silver threads. Nos 58 to 61 shown in figure 131 are examples, but individual reels cannot be purchased. There are strict conditions, so write for information.

The Royal School of Needlework
5 King Street
Covent Garden
London
WC2E 8HN
All embroidery materials. Also gold, Nos 29 to 47 as shown in figure 131.

Watts and Company Limited
Church furnishers
7 Tufton Street
London SW1
Cloth of gold and substitutes. Indian and other silks, cords, braids, etc.

John and Jenny Kilbride
Ditchling Common
Hassocks
Sussex
Weavers of 150 cm wide silk, and cotton and silk mixtures, in liturgical colours. These fabrics hang perfectly.

Liberty and Company Limited
Regent Street
London W1
Oriental silks including Thai. Other dress and furnishing fabrics.

Reeves-Dryad Limited
178 Kensington High Street
London W8 6SH
Felts, pattern drafting paper.

Sekers fabrics can be obtained through furnishing departments of large stores

R D Franks
Kent House
Market Place
London W1
Pattern drafting paper.

For useful addresses see also *Embroidery* magazine published by The Embroiderers' Guild.

SUPPLIERS IN THE USA

Appleton Brothers of London
West Main Road
Little Compton
Rhode Island 02837

American Thread Corporation
90 Park Avenue
New York NY 10016

Bucky King Embroideries Unlimited
121 South Drive
Pittsburgh
Pa 15238

Lily Mills
Shelby
North Carolina 28150

The Makings
1916 University Avenue
Berkeley
California 95704

The Needle's Point Studio
7013 Duncraig Court
McLean
Virginia 22101

The Rusty Needle
1479 Glenneyre
Laguna Beach
California 92651

The Sun Shop
7722 Maple Street
New Orleans
La 70118

INDEX

Numerals in *italics* refer to pages on which illustrations appear